The Conservation Easement Stewardship Guide

Designing, Monitoring, and Enforcing Easements

Brenda Lind

Land Trust Alliance, Washington, D.C.
Trust for New Hampshire Lands, Concord, New Hampshire
with assistance from the National Trust for Historic Preservation

Printed in the United States of America.

First printing.

For information, address the Land Trust Alliance, 900 Seventeenth Street NW, Suite 410, Washington, D.C. 20006. (202) 785-1410.

Library of Congress Cataloging-in-Publication Data

Lind, Brenda, 1960-
The conservation easement stewardship guide: designing, monitoring, and enforcing easements / Brenda Lind.
p. cm.
ISBN 0-943915-07-4 (pbk.) : $11.00
1. Servitudes—United States. 2. Land trusts—United States. 3. Conservation of natural resources—Law and legislation—United States. I. Land Trust Alliance. II. Trust for New Hampshire Lands. III. Title.
KF658.C65L56 1991
346.7304'35—dc20
[347.306435] 91-16150
CIP

Printed on Recycled Paper

Contents

Acknowledgments

This guide is a joint publication of the Land Trust Alliance and the Trust for New Hampshire Lands. Brenda Lind, Land Agent for TNHL, developed the outline and wrote the guide. The Land Trust Alliance established the review panel and solicited comments, reviewed and edited the manuscript, and coordinated production.

Additions to the guide relating to historic preservation easements were made by Stefan Nagel, Assistant General Counsel and Easement Program Administrator for the National Trust for Historic Preservation. We are grateful to the National Trust for the generous donation of his time and expertise, which greatly expands the audience for and usefulness of this publication.

This project was made possible by generous grants from several individuals and foundations. The National Fish and Wildlife Foundation provided a challenge grant, which was matched by contributions from the Ellis L. Phillips Foundation, Mr. Leslie Hubbard, Ms. Nancy P. Hayden, and the Trust for New Hampshire Lands. We are very grateful for their support.

Panel of Reviewers

The following individuals generously contributed their time and expertise to review drafts of this guide. Their thoughtful comments and suggestions have been incorporated in the discussion and have greatly enhanced its accuracy and scope of content. We extend our special thanks to Darby Bradley, Preston Bristow, and Kingsbury Browne who did detailed reviews of second and third drafts. Any inaccuracies are the responsibility of the author and publishers.

Mary Ellen Boelhower, Land Protection Specialist
Society for the Protection of New Hampshire Forests

Preston J. Bristow, Jr., Stewardship Director
Vermont Land Trust

Thomas Hahn, Associate Director
Open Lands Project/CorLands (Illinois)

Joel A. Lerner, Director, Division of Conservation Services
Massachusetts Executive Office of Environmental Affairs

Bob Myhr, Executive Director
The San Juan Preservation Trust (Washington)

Stefan Nagel, Assistant General Counsel and Easement
Program Administrator
National Trust for Historic Preservation

Caroline Norden, Director of Land Stewardship
Maine Coast Heritage Trust

Eric Olson, Office of the General Counsel
U.S. Department of Agriculture, Washington, D.C.

JoAnne Ruscio, Management Assistant
New Jersey Natural Lands Trust

Dennis Shaffer, Executive Director
Green Mountain Club (Vermont)
(formerly Administrator, Trust for Appalachian Trail Lands)

David M. Sherman, Lands Staff
U.S. Forest Service, Washington, D.C.

David D. Shields, Senior Land Planner
Brandywine Conservancy (Pennsylvania)

James B. Snow, Deputy Assistant General Counsel
Natural Resources Division, Office of General Counsel
U.S. Department of Agriculture, Washington, D.C.

Marjory M. Swope, Executive Director
New Hampshire Association of Conservation Commissions

James Turner, Forester
Mark Twain National Forest, Missouri

Joan Vilms, Consultant
Sonoma Land Trust (California)

Wesley T. Ward, Director, Land Conservation Center
The Trustees of Reservations (Massachusetts)

Charles D. Wyman, Land Protection Specialist
The Trustees of Reservations (Massachusetts)

LEGAL REVIEW

Darby Bradley, Esq., President
Vermont Land Trust

Kingsbury Browne, Esq.
Hill & Barlow, Boston

Land Trust Standards and Practices

The Land Trust Standards and Practices, developed by the Land Trust Alliance, outline the basic elements that the Alliance believes are essential for the responsible operation of a land trust—a land trust that operates legally, ethically, and in the public interest and that conducts a sound program of land transactions and stewardship. The Standards and Practices are meant to help new land trusts set up firm foundations on which to grow and to help existing land trusts review and improve the quality of their operations. For all land trusts, the Standards and Practices provide a tool for assuring landowners, donors, and public agencies of the soundness of the land trust's work.

The Standard, and accompanying Practices, for conservation easement stewardship are provided here (as they will appear in a revised 1992 version). They also can be applied to public agencies. The spirit and substance of the Standards are incorporated throughout *The Conservation Easement Stewardship Guide.*

Standard 14: Conservation Easement Stewardship

A land trust must carry out a program of responsible stewardship for its easements.

Practices

A. The land trust determines the financial and management implications of each transaction and establishes that it has or can raise the funds needed to monitor and enforce the easement.

B. The land trust monitors its conservation easement properties regularly, at least annually, in a manner appropriate to the size and restrictions of each property, and keeps documentation (reports, photographs, maps, etc.) of each monitoring visit.

C. The land trust informs new owners of easement-restricted properties about the easement's existence and restrictions and makes grantees and new owners aware of its monitoring policies.

D. The land trust enforces the terms of its conservation easements and takes necessary steps to see that violations are resolved.

E. The land trust makes contingency provisions for its easements in the event the trust ceases to exist or can no longer monitor them.

Introduction

From its inception only a few decades ago, the conservation easement has become a tremendously popular tool enabling the permanent protection of conservation land and historic property across the nation. Conservation easements protect more than five million acres nationwide. But as conservation easement acreage increases, so does the easement holders' responsibility to make sure that these easements last over time.

This guide is intended to be a step-by-step handbook to help conservation easement holders design and implement effective stewardship programs. It shares the experience and accepted stewardship practices of experienced easement holders nationwide. It is intended primarily for use by private land trusts and other conservation organizations as well as public agencies, but also has substantial application, and incorporates specific information, for historic preservation easements. It can help easement holders set up a stewardship program for the first time, or improve one they already have in place.

The Conservation Easement Stewardship Guide is a companion to *The Conservation Easement Handbook,* published by the Land Trust Alliance and the Trust for Public Land in 1988. It updates and considerably expands on the information in the *Handbook*. The *Handbook* provides an overview of stewardship topics, but this guide provides the additional detail needed to help set up a comprehensive program and carry it out on the ground. The *Handbook* includes a few additional sample documents, and a model conservation easement, that may be useful to easement stewardship programs. The Land Trust Alliance also can provide additional sample forms and policies to supplement the examples provided in this guide.

This guide describes the best combined stewardship practices of experienced easement holders nationwide. No single easement holder practices all the techniques described. Easement stewardship programs are individually tailored to the needs of the easement holder, property owner, easement terms, and type of resource. But whatever the individual circumstances, this guide can be used to develop a stewardship program that at a minimum meets basic standards—as well as one that is state-of-the-art in its scope and completeness.

Many easement holders using this guide will be just starting out—either just beginning to accept easements, or just beginning to design or improve a stewardship program for easements they've held for several years. Be aware that it takes thought, planning, and time to develop an effective stewardship program. Don't feel discouraged if you don't already have a comprehensive stewardship program in place, and don't feel pressured to do everything all at once. It has taken years of experience for the easement holders to put together the kinds of programs described in this guide. Set a schedule to gradually address and implement your own stewardship practices.

Conservation easements will only succeed as a conservation tool in the coming decades if each easement holder develops a sound stewardship program. Now that we know conservation easements work, we must work together to demonstrate that conservation easements can endure.

CHAPTER 1

Overview

A conservation easement, no matter how expertly crafted, cannot alone protect important land or historic resources—only the easement holder's excellent stewardship can. Acquiring an easement is just the beginning of the protection effort. Your ongoing commitment to monitor, defend, and enforce the easement is what ensures protection in perpetuity.

Why Stewardship?

Sound easement stewardship includes:

- *Thoughtful easement drafting.* A clear, legally defensible deed lays the foundation for effective stewardship.
- *Regular and documented monitoring.* Regular, documented inspection of the property identifies and resolves easement problems before they become serious violations.
- *Maintaining good relationships with the property owner and the community.* Good working partnerships are a vital tool to help protect the property.
- *Strong financial planning.* You must plan to have the funds to monitor and enforce the easement, in court if necessary.
- *A commitment to enforce the easement.* Only with a willingness to act against violations, including legal action if necessary, can an easement holder finally assure that resources are protected—or restored when damaged.

Effective stewardship can prevent problems from developing, as well as deal with them when they occur. By regularly monitoring your easements, and maintaining a working relationship with the property owner, you will frequently spot and resolve potential problems early on. If you ignore routine stewardship responsibilities, you risk major violations that seriously damage the basic conservation purposes of the easement.

Effective stewardship fosters good public relations. By upholding your promise to protect a property, you build credibility in the community for your easement program. A sound reputation for stewardship strengthens the confidence of the property owner—and other owners who might be contemplating protecting their property with an easement—that the property will remain protected. Healthy public support also can translate into financial support.

Stewardship is more than a practical way to ensure that conservation easements last: it is an ethical and legal responsibility. You must take care of your easements to honor your organizational mission. In addition, an organization that accepts tax-deductible easements must have the commitment and resources to enforce the easement in order to be a qualified donee under Internal Revenue Service regulations; failure to enforce your easements could render you ineligible to receive tax-deductible easement gifts.

TRUST FOR NEW HAMPSHIRE LANDS

The easement holder's governing body is responsible for easement stewardship; property visits help familiarize board members with what those obligations entail.

Setting Up a Stewardship Program

It is the responsibility of the organization's governing body to ensure that the organization conducts an adequate stewardship program for its easements. The governing body may assign the detailed development and implementation of the program to staff, a subcommittee, or volunteers, but it nevertheless must be accountable for the level and quality of stewardship. It should review and approve all stewardship policies.

To begin a stewardship program, or to make improvements to an existing one, review the scope of stewardship responsibilities described in this guide, and then take the following steps.

1. Assign overall responsibility for the stewardship program. Decide who—the board, a subcommittee, or staff—will be responsible for designing and implementing the program. Develop the chain of command, including who will perform detailed baseline documentation and monitoring tasks, who will oversee the process, and who will develop, design, and amend the stewardship program and present it to the governing body.

2. Establish procedures, standards, and policies for the stewardship program. Decide on procedures for developing baseline documentation, performing monitoring, handling violations, responding to property owner requests for amendments, and meeting other stewardship needs as they arise. Establish standards for the level and quality of these stewardship activities, including recordkeeping. Consider setting formal policies on how amendments, violations, and other special situations will be handled.

When possible, put policies, procedures, and standards in writing. This helps the organization be consistent and thorough in its stewardship activities. Written information also helps to inform property owners and the public about the easement holder's operations and commitment to stewardship.

3. Ensure adequate funding for the stewardship program. Determine how to pay for stewardship activities over time, including legal enforcement.

4. Provide for continuity. Make sure the stewardship program is incorporated into the organizational framework, so that it continues regardless of changes in administration. Sound stewardship, like the land it protects, endures.

Using foresight and initiative, you must do your best to develop and implement a stewardship program that defends the conservation resources of the property in perpetuity. But your stewardship program will also need to be occasionally reviewed and updated. Experience with conservation easements is only a few decades old and is rapidly evolving; stewardship programs need to be flexible to adapt to new lessons, ideas, and developments. As easement holders gain experience, they continually upgrade and revise their stewardship programs.

Try to keep in touch with other easement programs in your area and region, as well as with information sources like the Land Trust Alliance. While this guide presents current thinking about easement stewardship at the time of its writing, your most valuable resource will be your own experience and that of your colleagues.

CHAPTER 2

Before Accepting an Easement

Sound conservation easement stewardship begins before acquisition—by selecting easements wisely and drafting them to stand the test of time. Don't let the excitement of a promising acquisition sweep aside foresight. In the words of Tom Hahn of CorLands, a Chicago land trust, "After the glamour of acceptance, the ongoing liability of monitoring begins."

Holding conservation easements *is* a liability. Monitoring and record keeping takes time and, for most organizations, money. Dealing with violations—and especially going to court—requires even greater resources. Careful selection of potential conservation easement projects and thoughtful drafting will save you headaches down the road and make effective stewardship easier.

Selecting Easements

Organizations put considerable work and careful thought into deciding whether to accept an easement and negotiating its terms. During this process, be sure to consider the long-term stewardship responsibility the easement will entail. Before accepting a conservation easement, consider these questions:

1. Does the resource merit protection? All easement holders should have clear protection goals and criteria to evaluate potential projects. You want to avoid being saddled with permanent stewardship responsibilities for properties that are not truly important or do not meet acceptable standards. For tax-deductible easements, the easement should meet the "conservation purposes" tests of the IRS regulations. (Many easement holders use the IRS criteria as a basis for assessing all their easements.)

See *The Conservation Easement Handbook* for further discussion of easement selection criteria. The Land Trust Alliance can provide samples of project criteria used by land trusts around the country.

2. Is an easement sufficient to protect the property? Consider whether the conservation objectives for the property can be met using easement restrictions, or whether some other protection method would work better. For example, if the easement is intended to protect critical habitat for an endangered species, can it be crafted to provide adequate protection of the habitat? Or will only the management control afforded by fee ownership maintain the habitat?

3. How likely are violations or encroachments from surrounding land? Consider the surrounding land uses and local attitudes toward protecting the property. Is the easement particularly threatened by abutting land uses or third parties? An open space easement on property in a development with multiple residential abutters might suffer numerous violations along its boundaries. An easement located next to an industrial area may be subject to pollution that could damage the property's conservation values. A power line right-of-way may provide easy public access and likely abuse.

4. Is there another easement holder that is better able to protect the conservation values of the property? If you lack expertise in habitat evaluation, for example, you might not want to accept an easement intended to protect critical wildlife habitat, but instead to refer it to an organization with the appropriate expertise. Easements protecting historic structures are best monitored by an easement holder with architectural expertise. (If another appropriate holder is not available or preferable, you might decide to accept the easement, but to secure specialized monitoring expertise when needed.) An organization located closer to the easement or that holds adjacent property might be the most appropriate long-term steward. The goal should be to efficiently, effectively protect important resources—by whomever is best able and qualified to do so.

5. Are you capable of monitoring the easement? Geographic proximity and good physical access to the protected property generally make monitoring much easier. Consider whether size, distance, or remoteness of the property will make monitoring impractical.

6. Are you prepared to monitor all specific rights reserved by the property owner? If a landowner retains the right to build and subdivide residences within an easement, you must be prepared to review the proposed exercise of these rights to avoid easement violations. Easements on historic properties typically allow some modifications to structures with the prior approval of the easement holder. Such reviews take time, money, and expertise. Either you must have professional staff qualified to make this determination, or you will need to use outside specialists.

MAINE COAST HERITAGE TRUST

An easement that provides public access in a relatively developed area, like this shoreline access easement in Harpswell, Maine, may need frequent monitoring to be sure the access area remains unlittered and safe.

7. Does the easement entail substantial legal liability? The liability of an easement holder is not clear. While it stands to reason that holding an easement carries less liability risk than fee ownership of property, there is little legal evidence from the courts to support this. Generally, it seems that the more affirmative rights or management control the easement holder accepts—such as resource management, participation in farm operation, or oversight of public access—the greater its liability exposure. You may want to consult counsel to assess your potential liability exposure when such rights are to be included in an easement.

Hazardous wastes pose a particularly troublesome liability issue. Under the Superfund Act (formally the federal Comprehensive Environmental Response Compensation and Liability Act or CERCLA) and many state hazardous waste laws, current or prior owners of a contaminated property are potentially responsible for the costs of investigating and undertaking the clean-up. But whether easement holders are potentially liable is unclear. If there seems a reasonable likelihood that the property is contaminated with hazardous or toxic wastes, or could be contaminated in the future, you must carefully assess whether it is worth the risk of getting involved with the property. You should take appropriate steps prior to easement acquisition to discover such contamination, in order to help avoid being held liable if such contamination is found in the future. Contact the Land Trust Alliance for more information on hazardous waste liability.

8. Are you prepared to do any property management that is required by the easement or by a separate agreement with the property owner? Some easement holders are willing to accept certain management responsibilities that are necessary to preserve or protect the conservation values of the easement property—for example, managing endangered species habitat or overseeing public access. If you accept affirmative management responsibilities in the easement—or through a side agreement with the owner—consider whether you have the expertise, time, and money needed to meet management obligations.

9. Does the property owner have clear title? Be sure a property owner has clear title on which to grant the easement, either by buying title insurance or by thoroughly checking the legal background of the property. A professional title opinion or report can make sure that any mortgages or liens on the property have been properly released or subordinated. It should also discover other potential encumbrances that may affect the conservation values of the property, such as third party mineral rights or a forgotten right-of-way. A clouded title can threaten the easement holder's ability to enforce the restrictions, or even the validity of the easement itself.

10. Do you have, or can you raise, adequate funds to monitor and enforce the easement? Carrying out easement stewardship activities in perpetuity is a significant financial commitment. If you are unprepared to finance stewardship costs—especially in the case of an easement with complex monitoring requirements (such as development approvals) or high potential for violations—you should refer the easement to another capable easement holder. (See Chapter 7 for further discussion of financing stewardship.)

Easement holders can and do refuse easements when monitoring and defending the easement would be unacceptably difficult or expensive. One land trust, for example, refused an easement on land threatened with eminent domain proceedings, in order to avoid a politically and financially expensive court battle. Another refused an easement on land located in a developed subdivision, judging that its conservation value had already been diminished and that its protection would require more monitoring than the trust could provide.

Drafting Monitorable and Enforceable Easements

Imagine trying to interpret and enforce a conservation easement that says, "No mining is allowed." Would topsoil removal or sod farming be allowed? An easement's restrictions must be monitorable and enforceable, and they must be supported by a clear statement of the easement's purpose. Future interpretation of the easement rests on how clearly the document explains the restrictions and their intent, as well as on how enforceable the restrictions are.

Consider these recommendations while negotiating and drafting an easement.

1. Clearly state the purpose of the easement. Make sure that anyone who reads the document can tell exactly what the easement means to accomplish. David M. Sherman of the U.S. Forest Service provides this example: "The purpose of this easement is to preserve the view of the property as seen from Jefferson Rock in Harpers Ferry, West Virginia, in a wooded manner where no manmade improvements will be visible at any time during the year." If a new house is later constructed that is visible, a judge can tell it is clearly in violation of the original intent of the easement. Attorney Thomas S. Barrett, author of the "Model Conservation Easement" in *The Conservation Easement Handbook*, calls the purpose clause "the touchstone of the easement....If the easement is reasonably clear about the conservation values to be protected, it should provide a workable standard."

2. Clearly identify boundaries. You cannot monitor encroachments if you can't identify the exact location of easement boundaries on the ground. It is best to have a boundary survey to ensure that the easement boundaries are marked and the corners are pinned with permanent markers, and its metes and bounds should be written in the legal description of the easement. For special use areas, such as building envelopes where future structures will be allowed, it is best to identify the boundaries of the area at the time the easement is acquired, and those boundaries should be surveyed. Alternatively, you can require that a survey be done when the right is exercised later. If a survey is not practical, be sure to define the boundaries using identifiable, permanent points on the ground. Performance standards, such as a setback distance from a stream or highway, can also be used.

Boundary lines can be difficult to locate and must be marked clearly both on a map and on the ground prior to accepting the easement.

MAINE COAST HERITAGE TRUST

3. Use measurable standards. Suppose an easement is intended to protect scenic views across a pond to an undeveloped forested shoreline. Don't simply say, "No activities are allowed that would disturb the scenic view." Instead, define a linear setback from the shore and state specific activities that are restricted within the setback. Craft the standard so that compliance can be objectively measured. (For evaluating modifications or alterations to historic structures, the objective standard often used is the *Standards for Rehabilitation and Guidelines for Rehabilitating Historic Buildings*, issued by the U.S. Department of the Interior.)

4. If measurable standards are impractical, refer to accepted standards. For example, an easement allowing agriculture and forestry can specify that "forestry and agricultural management activities shall be in accordance with the current scientifically based practices recommended by the U.S. Cooperative Extension Service, U.S. Soil Conservation Service, or other government or private nonprofit natural resource conservation and management agencies then active" (Society for the Protection of New Hampshire Forests standard easement). The easement holder then has a reference point to use when evaluating questionable management. Such language gives flexibility if accepted practices change over time as the result of scientific advances and new technologies. On the other hand, such standards can be subjective and prone to conflicts of interpretation, so use them carefully.

5. For historic preservation easements, consider a rehabilitation agreement. Easements on historic structures on which rehabilitation work is to be performed may be supplemented with a "Rehabilitation Agreement," which is generally incorporated by reference in the easement document but may instead be incorporated in the document directly.

6. Avoid restrictions that cannot be monitored. For example, an easement holder should avoid restrictions prohibiting use of synthetic chemicals on an organic farm if it cannot measure and monitor chemical use. If it chooses to accept such restrictions in the easement, the easement holder must maintain especially close contact with the property owner to reduce the risk of violation.

7. Avoid unenforceable restrictions. An easement holder should avoid restrictions on activities that realistically cannot be enforced, like "No dogs may be unleashed" or "No motor vehicles are allowed." As a practical matter, you do not want to be in the position of trying to respond to unenforceable violations. Moreover, failure to enforce a restriction may render the restriction legally invalid. An alternative way to achieve some of the same results would be to require the property owner to take certain enforceable steps, such as posting the land, to prevent undesirable activities. For historic structures, it could require the property owner to perform maintenance at defined intervals.

8. Require grantee approval. For tax-deductible easements, the IRS requires that the donor must notify the easement holder in writing before exercising any reserved rights that may have an adverse impact on the conservation values protected by the easement. For any reserved rights with a high potential for causing easement violations, such as constructing roads or buildings, the easement should require not only notice but also the easement holder's *approval* before such rights may be exercised.

9. Legal review. You may provide an initial draft easement document based on your own model or one of those provided in *The Conservation Easement Handbook,* but you should affirmatively and in writing urge the potential easement grantor to receive independent legal counsel as well. You don't want later to be involved in any conflict of interest or misrepresentation allegations—which, among other things, could invalidate the easement.

Finally, consider the big picture. Does the easement protect what you want it to protect? Will it stand the test of time? New technologies? New owners? The terms must be flexible enough to allow unforseen activities that are consistent with the purposes of the easement, but strong and clear enough to prevent unacceptable activities. Attorney Stephen J. Small suggests applying the following test:

> Conservation-minded land trusts work with conservation-minded landowners to produce an easement document that sounds beautiful. But take the defensive perspective. Read it as if you were the lawyer representing the next landowner, who is hostile to the easement, and who instructs the lawyer, "Read this and tell me what I can get away with."

One public official with many years of easement experience warns:

> To enforce an easement, ambiguity must be eliminated to the maximum extent possible. I've had 20 years experience with easements, and I am firmly convinced that the human animal is never more creative than when it is to his economic advantage to try to get around the terms of an easement.

Draft with the hostile property owner in mind.

CHAPTER 3

Baseline Documentation

Baseline documentation records the condition of the property at the time of the easement's acquisition. Some easement holders create a larger baseline file that provides an overall record of the property's history, how the easement was acquired, and other specialized information about the property or easement. Regardless of the extent of an easement holder's approach to baseline documentation, good baseline documentation is essential for the following reasons:

- *Baseline data provides evidence of conservation resource values.* You must have a thorough record of initial property conditions as proof of the resource values of the property. If you must defend the easement against a violation in court, baseline documentation shows that the alleged violation did not pre-date the easement.

- *Baseline data is required by the IRS for tax-deductible easement gifts.* IRS regulations require that the donor of an easement gift provide the easement holder with "documentation sufficient to establish the condition of the property at the time of the gift" if the donor has reserved rights that may, when exercised, impair the conservation value of the property. The regulations further require that, for any natural resource protected by the easement's restrictions, the condition of that resource at or near the time of the gift must be established. See Appendix B for IRS regulations pertaining to baseline documentation.

- *Baseline documentation provides a summary file for organizational use.* It is useful to expand the baseline file to include information on why the easement was granted, acquisition history, the organization's relationship with the donor, legal encumbrances, and the like. A thorough baseline file can be used by easement monitors, new stewardship personnel, and others to efficiently learn about or review significant features of the easement property.

Who Documents?

The conservation easement holder generally prepares the baseline documentation or arranges for its preparation. If the easement is a tax-deductible gift, and if the donor retains rights in the property that, once exercised, could impair the conservation values of that property, the IRS holds the *donor* responsible for providing the baseline data. As a practical matter, however, the easement holder is best able to ensure that all the information necessary to manage and enforce the easement is assembled and organized in an easily referenced format.

Baseline documentation can often be developed by trained laypeople. However, specialists may be required in some situations. For example, an architect may be needed to document the exact condition of a historic facade, or an ecologist may be needed to document the condition of a fragile habitat.

When to Document

For tax-deductible easements, the IRS regulations require the donor to provide the documentation *prior to the time the donation is made,* in order to establish the property's condition at the time of the gift—and this is generally a wise approach for all easements, whether or not a tax-deduction is sought. Many easement holders also upgrade and add information to the baseline file later, dating the new information to show that it was added after the acquisition.

Contents of the Baseline Documentation File

At a minimum, the file should include two items:

- *Documentation of the property's conservation values,* especially those likely to be affected by each restriction and reserved right contained in the easement. Details on documenting conservation values are discussed below.

- *Acknowledgment statement.* The IRS requires that for tax-deductible easements, both the donor and donee must sign a statement referencing the baseline file and acknowledging that it is an accurate representation of the property's condition at the time of its transfer. This requirement makes good sense for all easements, since it will help establish the accuracy of evidence presented in the baseline file in a court of law.

TRUST FOR NEW HAMPSHIRE LANDS

Baseline documentation should include photos of buildings that are within the easement area to document their present location, size, appearance, and use.

Other useful information for an easement holder to collect and maintain in the baseline documentation file include:

- *Cover sheet,* outlining the contents of the file.

- *Directions to the property.*

- *Easement summary.* A one-page easement summary that includes a statement of the purpose of the easement, a list of restrictions and reserved rights, ownership, and recording information gives a quick overview of the easement that is especially useful in the field. See Appendix C for a sample easement summary form.

- *Legal information.* Include the recorded easement document and title report, if available. It is especially important to have documentation of any other legal encumbrances on the property, such as abutter rights-of-way, water rights, etc.

- *Property owner information.* Develop a narrative or a descriptive "timeline" summarizing the history of the easement's acquisition and contacts with the property owner. This information will be very useful to future monitors, who may need to know these details when meeting with the property owner.

See the Baseline Data Checklist and Sample Easement Documentation Form in Appendices D and E.

Documenting Conservation Values

Baseline data should document in detail the condition of all ecological, scenic, historic, geologic, land use, and other property features that are protected or affected by the easement terms. The baseline documentation need not contain a comprehensive description of every property feature—collecting unnecessary detail wastes time and money—but it should document the specific property conditions that are the subject of the easement. For tax-deductible easements, see the IRS regulations on baseline documentation (see Treas. Reg. § 1.170A-14(g)(5)(i)).

The volume and specificity of the baseline documentation will vary depending on the particulars of the easement. The more specific or restrictive the easement's terms, the more in-depth and specific the documentation needs to be. The documentation should be descriptive, including detailed maps and plans, photos, architectural depictions for historic structures, or narratives (see below). The documentation should be objective and reproducible, so that a person monitoring the property or documenting a violation can repeat the baseline documentation methods in the future. The goal is to provide a common reference point for future inspections and a baseline of conditions to demonstrate the existence and extent of any violations.

Using Maps and Plans

Baseline documentation should include appropriate maps and plans at different scales to show the location of the easement as well as specific property characteristics. Some examples:

- Show the property location with the boundaries outlined on a U.S. Geological Survey topographic map or other regional map.

- Show features such as boundary markers, roads, trails, water courses, buildings, or other improvements on a property survey map or other detailed map. Show any areas of special land use, or locations of important features affected by the easement, such as special ecological or historic features. When finished, your detailed map probably will be covered with added notes and sketched-in features. This will help future interpreters of the baseline file to understand the property.

- For historic structures, show a floor plan of the building.

Using Photos

Photos—either aerial or ground—are a quick, relatively inexpensive, and very effective tool for documenting a property's condition.

Aerial photos. For open space properties, obtain a low-altitude aerial photo of the property and map the property boundaries on it. Many easement holders report that this is the most useful element of the file.

Place lines on aerial photos to clearly show the property location and boundaries.

It helps monitors find the boundaries, and is an excellent tool from which to track land use changes or violations. For assistance in obtaining aerial photos, contact regional offices of the Soil Conservation Service (U.S. Department of Agriculture) or local county conservation district offices.

Ground photos. Take photos to generally document the condition of the property and to specifically document any special protected features or areas affected by the owner's reserved rights. Photograph all structures, utilities, and manmade improvements on the property. Take pictures along boundary lines and at property corners; this shows adjacent land use and will help future monitors find the property boundaries. Some open space easement holders report that abutters have dug up and moved boundary markers in an effort to encroach on an easement without detection. Baseline boundary photos help secure the record.

It is a good idea to establish permanent photo points so that photos will be easy to interpret and replicate in the future. Choose points that will be easy to locate, such as road or trail intersections. When taking the shot, try to include permanent landmarks within the photo frame. Mark the photo point on a detailed photo point map. Label the photo with the subject, location, and orientation of the photo.

MAINE COAST HERITAGE TRUST

Document scenic views with photos taken at or near the public rights-of-way from which they may be seen.

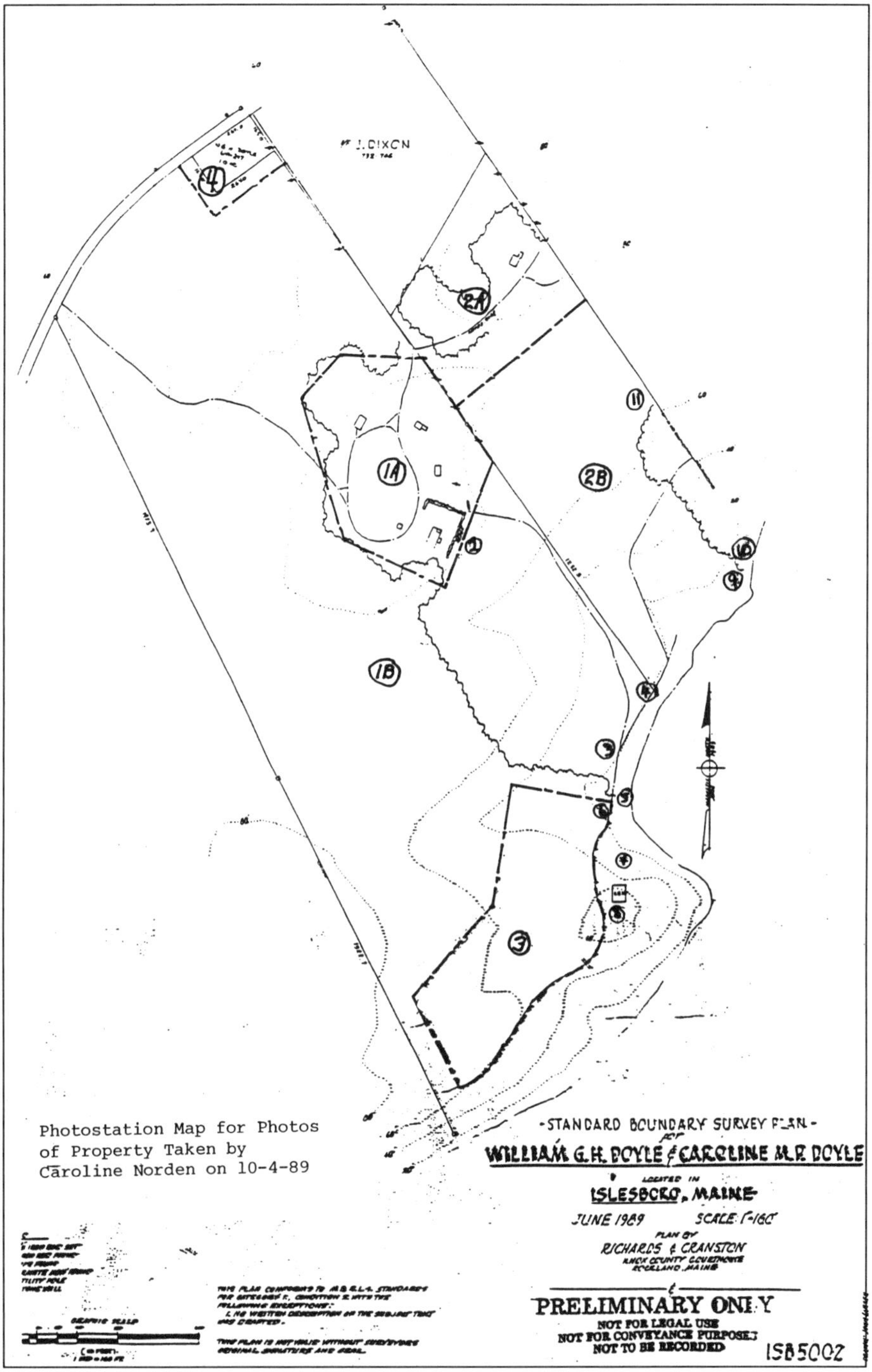

Prepare a photo location map to accompany the labeled photos.

Using Architectural Depictions

Structures that are very significant architecturally and that are protected by the easement should be depicted in architectural drawings, preferably meeting documentation standards of the Historic American Buildings Survey of the U.S. Department of the Interior.

Using Narratives

Use brief narrative descriptions as necessary to describe the easement features and supplement or explain information depicted on photos, maps, and drawings. The baseline file might include paragraphs summarizing the condition of key ecological, historic, or scenic features protected by the easement, for example. Explain any lists, tables, and measurements included in the baseline data. But keep in mind that this is primarily a legal, not a scientific document. Write descriptions according to professional standards, but in terms that the layperson can understand.

Examples of Support Documentation

For an easement that protects a scenic view from a public way, narratively describe what, specifically, can be seen. Take photos and label the subject, the point from which the photo was taken, and the orientation of the photo. File any official recognition of the view, such as its mention in a municipal master plan.

For an easement protecting critical wildlife habitat, document the habitat features with descriptive detail. List species and narratively describe habitat quality. Record measurements of the relevant vegetation, wetland characteristics, and level of wildlife species use. File evidence of any official recognition of the area.

For an easement protecting a historic structure, take photos of the structure, generally wide angle, and then photograph the specific protected elements. A written description of the property's condition, paying attention to signs of structural defects that may not be visible from photographs, is useful as well. File national, state, or local historical registry documentation that pertains to the property.

Storing Baseline Documentation

File the original baseline documentation in a safe storage place. Keep a copy of the file for use by monitors in a more easily accessible location.

Some easement holders record the baseline documentation with the easement in the deed registry, and re-record it if later additions to the baseline file are made. In jurisdictions that do not accept baseline file contents such as maps or photos, you can record the owner "acknowledgment of condition" referencing the baseline file. The registry of deeds provides safe archival storage for this material, and ensures that the information is on public record.

CHAPTER 4

Monitoring

The easement and the baseline documentation provide the basis for permanent property protection, but only your monitoring program—a program of regularly inspecting and documenting the condition of the property—ensures the property is protected over time. Regular and documented monitoring is essential for several reasons:

- *To catch violations.* Monitoring is an easement holder's chief tool to discover violations.
- *To build rapport with the property owner.* Monitoring offers an opportunity to develop a spirit of cooperation with the property owner. Through regular monitoring contact, you can educate the property owner, invite questions, discuss potential problems, defuse problems before they become serious, and avoid violations. Some easement holders report that through this contact, they have found that a property owner wants to strengthen the easement, or knows of other owners nearby who want to preserve their property. Good rapport can lead to additional gifts of money or property.
- *To save time and money.* Monitoring can detect a violation before it becomes so deeply entrenched, and the property owner so committed to an adversarial position, that only legal action can resolve the situation.
- *To provide a record in case of court action.* If a violation occurs and is brought to court, monitoring documentation helps establish that you are a responsible easement holder. It also provides a running record of the property's condition, which is essential to determine adequate restoration or resolution of the violation.

- *To satisfy Internal Revenue Service requirements for tax-deductible easements.* To qualify as an eligible easement donee, IRS regulations specify an organization must "have a commitment to protect the conservation purposes of the donation." (See Treas. Reg. 1.170-A-14(c)(1).) On the strength of this provision and others, the Internal Revenue Service could deem it necessary to review an easement holder's files to determine whether it regularly monitors its easements. A program of regular inspections will help to demonstrate the requisite "commitment" to the protection of the easement property.

This chapter discusses the procedures for doing the monitoring and documenting the results. The discussion outlines minimum guidelines and, where appropriate, describes various approaches to the specific design of a monitoring program. You should tailor your program to the type of property you are protecting, the easement restrictions, the size and framework of your organization, and your experience as an easement holder.

How Often to Inspect

Experienced easement holders recommend monitoring at least annually, eithier by visiting the property on the ground or inspecting it by air. Annual monitoring reminds the property owner of the easement's existence and helps you learn of any changes in ownership. Making monitoring an annual event ensures that you will regularly check the property's condition. The Land Trust Alliance's Land Trust Standards and Practices, which suggest minimum operating requirements for land trusts, specify that easements should be monitored annually.

Easement-encumbered properties with a greater potential for violation may need more frequent inspection. Such properties include the following:

Easements restricting or requiring repeated actions, such as a conservation easement that prohibits tilling on farmland abutting a water course. The property should be checked often enough to discover any violations and limit damage that could occur.

Easements with development or historic rehabilitation potential. Especially during construction or rehabilitation activities, these easements need frequent inspection to ensure that the activity occurs only as allowed.

Easements in heavily populated areas. Open space easements adjacent to residential developments, for example, have a greater potential to be abused and violated by trespassers. The same may be true of more remote easement properties that have been used as traditional "party spots." Illegal dumping can be an annoying problem; while it is generally the property owner's job to take care of the problem, you might want to inspect frequently to alert the landowner if problems are discovered.

Small easements or those with many abutters. Such easements may need more frequent inspections to check for boundary encroachments, such as residential neighbors dumping refuse over the boundary.

Easements with public access provisions. Depending on the type of access allowed and any maintenance responsibility the easement holder has accepted, these easements may require frequent inspection to check for hazardous conditions, vandalism, or abusive uses. Easements with posting provisions—for example, those allowing a landowner to post the land against hunting but not hiking—may need to be checked seasonally.

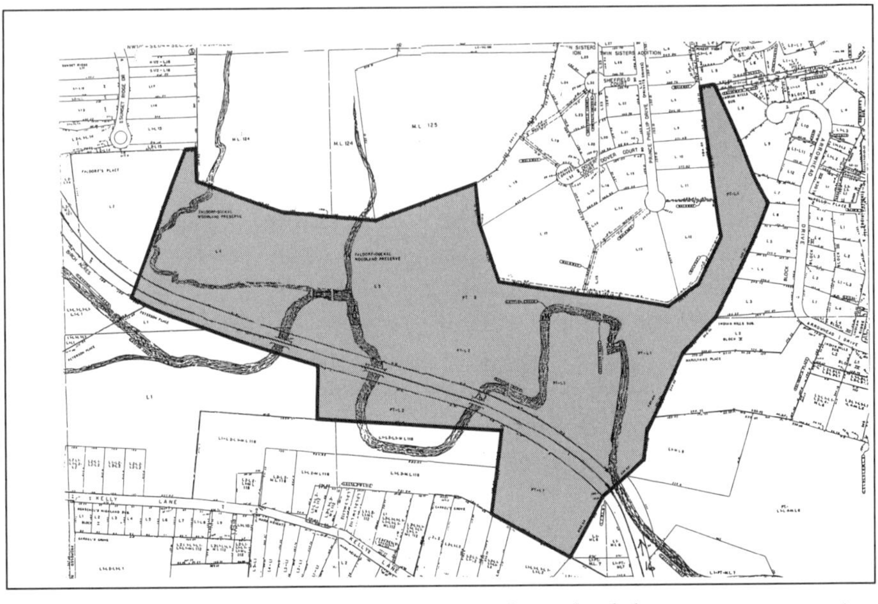

IOWA NATURAL HERITAGE FOUNDATION

An easement like this, which borders on residential subdivisions, may require more frequent monitoring to detect potential boundary encroachments.

Easements in which you have accepted any management rights or responsibilities. For example, if you have accepted responsibility for maintaining a threatened wildlife habitat by posting the land or managing the vegetation, you must inspect the property often enough to know the condition of the habitat.

Some easements holders with many easements rank their holdings according to level of risk and monitor "hot spots" that have a high potential for violation seasonally or even weekly. Another approach is to supplement annual monitoring of more vulnerable easement properties with frequent, informal monitoring "drive-bys."

Some easement holders perform formal monitoring only every three to five years on isolated, low vulnerability tracts, such as remote unmanaged woodland that is inaccessible by vehicle. Monitoring less than annually increases the likelihood that any violation will worsen. A regular, documented monitoring schedule becomes even more important if an organization chooses to monitor less than annually, to ensure that monitoring isn't overlooked on the years it is scheduled to occur. The Land Trust Alliance recommends annual monitoring for all properties.

Who Monitors?

Different people may do the monitoring, but one person needs to be in charge. This person must ensure that monitoring never slips through the cracks. This person should see that regular property inspections are completed, that reliable and accurate monitoring records are kept, and that property owners are regularly contacted. When this person leaves the organization, he or she must arrange to convey the monitoring duties to the next person in charge.

Monitors must be trained thoroughly, so they are familiar with the easement's terms, the appropriate points to inspect on the property, proper conduct for dealing with the property owner, and recordkeeping methods. Try to have the same person do the monitoring over several years, so he or she can build a personal rapport with the owner and gain familiarity with the particulars of the property. A pair of monitors working together is a good idea, since two pairs of eyes can see more than one.

Volunteers, interns, staff, consultants, or board members can perform monitoring duties. Larger, staffed organizations often assign one staff person who is familiar with the property and its restrictions and is experienced in resolving problems. Smaller organizations without trained staff sometimes contract with larger easement holders or consultants for monitoring services or assistance.

Some easement holders like using college interns, but point out that the lack of continuity from year to year can be a problem. Volunteers can be excellent monitors, especially if they live near the property and can visit it frequently. Using volunteers is a good way to involve the community as well. Some organizations like to use board members, which keeps monitoring in-house and keeps board members well-informed about property condition.

Designing an Easement Inspection Form

To keep a record of the property's condition that is easy to use and understand, design a standard inspection form that monitors can use for all properties. It must document that the property was inspected and whether it was found to be in compliance with the easement's terms. This form also can include other information to update the easement file, such as the property's general condition and management and information about the property owner. This form provides the legal documentation to substantiate your regular monitoring program. *Minimally*, the form should include:

- Current property owner name and address
- Location of property
- Method of inspection (personal visit, aerial view)
- Whether the property appears to be in compliance with the easement
- The name of the inspector, including signature and date

Inspection forms *also* can include:

- A summary of the easement's restrictions
- Other property owner information, such as phone number, local representative, owner's signature
- List of all people accompanying the monitor
- Brief description of the condition of the property
- Description of any manmade alteration of the property, including any reserved rights that have been exercised
- Description of any alterations due to natural causes
- Other observation or comments
- List of photos and maps accompanying the inspection report

See Appendix F for a sample inspection form.

Choosing a Monitoring Method: Ground or Aerial

You can monitor your easements by walking the property or by aerial observation, depending on the size and type of property and the specific easement terms. The pros and cons of each approach are briefly described here. Specific procedures for doing the monitoring are covered later in this chapter.

Ground monitoring is appropriate for easements small enough to be covered on foot. Ground monitoring is essential for restrictions that require close visual inspection—for example, restrictions on overgrazing that are measured by the condition and composition of forage or restrictions on uses to prevent disturbance to an endangered species. Easements that permit public access usually should be monitored on the ground. Most easement holders monitor on the ground.

Aerial monitoring is useful and cost-effective to monitor a very large easement or numerous small easements in a concentrated area. The U.S. Fish and Wildlife Service monitors its waterfowl management easements by air, as do several land trusts that hold extensive easement acreage.

Low altitude flight is the best way to thoroughly view the boundaries and interior of large or remote properties. It is the best way to observe activity on neighboring land, which may alert the easement holder to potential encroachments. However, it does require facility with maps and aerial photos, great familiarity with the landscape, and a strong flight stomach on the part of the monitor. It helps to have the same person do aerial monitoring each year, to capitalize on the monitor's experience. Whenever a violation is suspected, or aerial observation shows significant change in the property, the property must be monitored on the ground as well.

Satellite imagery may be a viable monitoring tool in the future, although at present the cost for high-resolution satellite photos is prohibitive.

Monitoring by boat. Easements protecting shoreline or islands may be monitored by boat. However, if the easement extends inland past the sight distance, additional ground or aerial monitoring is usually needed.

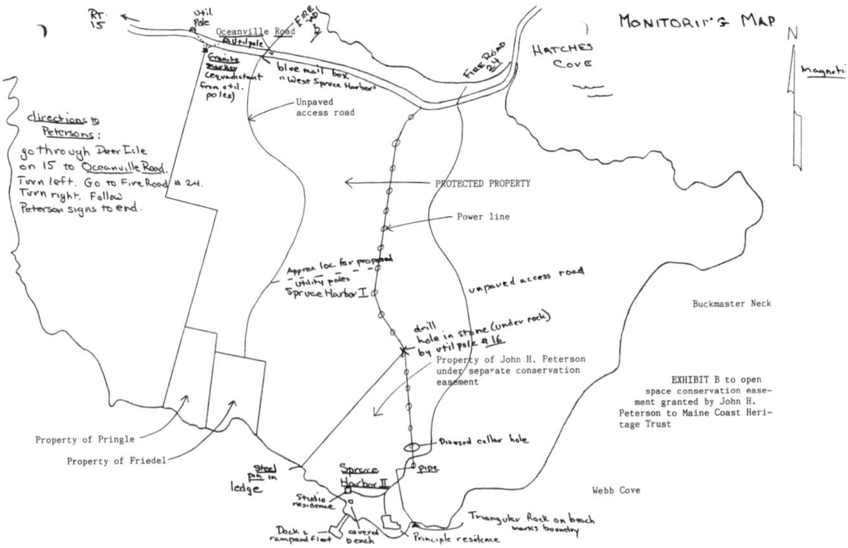

An annotated map showing property features and stored in the monitoring file will help future monitors find their way around the property.

Doing the Inspection

The steps for doing the monitoring vary somewhat depending on whether the monitoring is done by air or on the ground. The basic steps for both are outlined here.

Ground Monitoring

1. Schedule the visit. Contact the property owner well in advance and make every effort to schedule the visit at a time when the property owner can attend. (If building interiors will be inspected, the property owner or a designated representative must be present.) Including the property owner helps to establish a cooperative relationship. It also provides an opportunity to review the easement and address any questions or problems promptly. Some easement holders suggest sending a letter to property owners to remind them about the inspection, to briefly update them on the organization's activities and projects, and to provide an additional paper trail of the inspection in the easement holder's file.

For woodland properties, it's best to schedule the visit when leaves are off the trees to provide maximum visibility. Also, for visibility, avoid monitoring when snow is on the ground.

2. Review materials. A few days before the visit, familiarize yourself with the easement. Look over the baseline documentation file and the previous year's monitoring documentation. Review the easement and photos to refresh your memory of any special features or areas needing inspection. Make note of any new photos needed to bring the file up to date. Review letters, memos, and notes. You need to be knowledgeable about the easement's history and the organization's relationship with the owner in case the owner asks questions.

If the easement contains technical provisions requiring expert evaluation, arrange for that additional inspection. For example, if the easement contains a restriction referencing a specific water quality standard, you might need to obtain a water quality expert's opinion on whether that standard is being met.

3. Gather materials and equipment. For the visit, gather together:

- The easement document
- Easement summary (if one has been prepared)
- Most recent aerial photo with property boundaries mapped in, and/or recent ground photos
- USGS topographic or other relevant map with property boundaries mapped in
- Survey or other map which shows roads, waterways, improvements, and other property features
- Easement inspection form and note pad
- Camera
- Film (high-speed film works best in varied light conditions)
- Map showing established photo points, if any

It may also be useful to bring:

- Tape recorder to dictate property observations
- Video camera (can be used in place of a camera and tape recorder)
- Flagging
- Field tape measure
- Compass
- Field copy of the property baseline and monitoring documentation file for reference

4. Review the easement with the property owner. If the property owner can be present, it's a good idea to first sit down together and review the easement. Go over its purposes and terms. Review the monitoring procedure and encourage the owner to join you for the physical inspection. If appropriate, discuss any property management questions you or the owner may have. Update the owner about your organization's recent activities or accomplishments in the region. Invite questions.

MAINE COAST HERITAGE TRUST

When monitoring, walk the boundary lines of a property to check for encroachments from neighboring properties.

5. Walk the boundaries. Walk the entire property boundary if possible. Cumbersome though this may seem, experienced easement holders report that many violations occur at the boundaries, caused by trespassing by adjacent property owners. If property size, topography, or remoteness make it impractical to walk the boundaries, be sure to visit those boundaries that are easily accessible to the public. Boundaries are especially vulnerable to trespasser abuses such as trash disposal. Often the owner won't even know about these encroachments, so boundary inspection is vital. Encourage the owner to maintain the boundaries by brushing them out or by other appropriate means.

TRUST FOR NEW HAMPSHIRE LANDS

Monitoring should document areas with special restrictions. For an easement that protects undeveloped water frontage, make a point to inspect and document the condition of the shoreline.

6. Inspect the property interior. For open space easements, you may not need to inspect the entire property, but do visit major land use areas and suspected problem areas. Focus on areas affected by special easement restrictions or rights reserved by the owner. For example, if an easement prohibits cutting trees within 100 feet of a pond, make a point to visit and inspect the waterfront. Be sure to visit informal public use areas, such as camping, picnicking, or party spots, and areas accessible by motorized vehicle. If the easement provides public access, specifically check access areas to make sure they are open and safe.

The inspection of historic preservation easements on structures may require periodic inspection of interior spaces, even if the easement covers only the facade, to assure that structural integrity is maintained.

7. Document current conditions. Compare the current property condition with the written observations and photos from the previous monitoring visit. Make special note of any major changes, such as damages from insect infestation, storms, or other natural occurrences. Thoroughly document with notes and photos any manmade improvements to the property. Photograph major changes in property condition or land use. Photograph boundaries if there are major changes in abutting property use. Use established photo points if possible, and note new photo points on the map. Keep a written log of photo locations if necessary. If you use a video camera, verbally describe your location and special features being recorded. Fill out the inspection form, or make sure you have adequate information to do so later.

8. Identify and document violations. Identify potential violations by comparing the property condition with the exact terms of the easement. If a questionable activity or potential violation exists, follow up by documenting the situation and contacting the property owner. See Chapter 6 for further information on identifying and documenting violations.

Aerial Monitoring

1. Schedule the flight. As with ground monitoring, choose a time of maximum visibility. Check with an aerial mapping company in your state for more information about your region's best aerial photograph season.

Choose a pilot who is familiar with the local landscape and has experience with aerial photography if possible. The pilot can make your job much easier if he or she can help locate the property and position the plane at the correct angle and height for good aerial photos. It is best to use a plane with wings above, not below, the side window, for maximum visibility. You may take photos out of the passenger window, opened if possible, or a floor window, if the plane is so equipped.

2. Review easement materials. Before the flight, gather and review the easement materials as you would for ground monitoring. Especially familiarize yourself with previous aerial photographs with the boundary outlined, noting roads, buildings, and property features that will help orient you. It can be very difficult to identify the property from the air, and it may be necessary for the monitor to visit the property and view the boundaries and landmarks on the ground first.

Pre-flight organization is key to a successful monitoring flight. Preston Bristow of the Vermont Land Trust advises, "The tight, bouncing cockpit of a single engine plane is not the place to be pawing through files or rolling out maps. Flight books in ring binders are recommended." Appropriate preparation for motion sickness helps, too.

MAINE COAST HERITAGE TRUST

When monitoring by air, take new aerial photos as needed to document significant changes on the easement property or new abutting land uses.

3. Fly the easement. Locate the property boundaries and check whether any adjacent land use may have encroached onto the property. Observe the property interior and compare the current property condition with the previous aerial photograph. Take time to have the pilot position the plane at the best altitude and orientation for photographs, if any are needed. Photograph major changes in the condition of the property, areas of suspected violation, and new manmade improvements.

4. Assess the need for ground inspection. If you detect a possible violation, major new improvements, or significant changes in the land use or vegetation, you should follow up with a ground inspection to document the changes. Even if no inspection is necessary, you should plan to meet with the property owner periodically to review the easement (see Chapter 5 for further discussion).

Documentation: Leaving a Paper Trail

Back in the office, fill out, sign, and date the easement inspection form. Label photos with the subject, date, and location from which the photo was taken, and sign them. Mark any new photo points on the map. Sign and date all new maps and notes that are added to the easement file. Make sure all the easement inspection documentation is filed and stored in accordance with good recordkeeping practices. See Appendix A for a general discussion of recordkeeping practices.

Send the property owner a friendly letter confirming that the property was inspected. (Use this opportunity to convey any other messages, too, such as reminding the owner to tell you if the property is sold or transferred.) Some easement holders send a copy of the inspection report to the property owner and to any leaseholders for the property. Some have the property owner sign and return copies of the letter, the inspection report, and copies of any new photographs taken to acknowledge their awareness that the property has been monitored and that the inspection report and photos correctly document its condition. File the letter and other material with the inspection report.

Some easement holders annually file monitoring inspection reports or a summary statement about them in local deed registries. This ensures that the public record will show that the easement holder did its job, even 50 or 100 years down the road.

Review and Approval of Reserved Rights

If you have accepted an easement with reserved rights that require your approval before the landowner exercises them, such as construction of buildings, then you must plan for the time and money required to meet this additional monitoring responsibility. Some easement holders find that they spend more time reviewing and inspecting requests for approval than doing their regular monitoring, particularly for easements that allow limited development.

Because so many variables occur during construction, it is especially important to inspect the property frequently if buildings are approved. It is much easier to address and correct potential easement violations or misunderstandings during construction than later, when the protected resource may already be irreparably damaged. Wesley Ward, of The Trustees of Reservations, warns: "It may be extremely difficult to convince a court to order removal of a building already constructed."

If you accept easements with reserved rights needing review, you should design the review process ahead of time. Design a fair process, and put it in writing. This should help discourage the owner from exerting undue pressure on you to make concessions. The review process can be written into the easement document or kept as a separate written policy.

- Decide who will be responsible for receiving the request, reviewing the specific easement terms, compiling needed background information, and doing a site visit.
- Determine whether staff, a board subcommittee, or the full board will make the approval decision.
- Develop a system for documenting the request, the review process, and the decision, so that a "paper trail" exists for future reference. Thorough documentation will help the organization be consistent in future approval requests. (A sample approval form is included in Appendix G.)

Follow up approvals with inspections, to make sure that what was approved is what actually occurs. It may be useful to meet with the individuals performing the work—for example, the construction manager or architect for buildings, the forester for sensitive logging jobs—to be sure they understand the easement restrictions. Again, leave a paper trail; document inspections, results, and your final sign-off when the work is complete.

CHAPTER 5

Property Owner and Community Relations

In the long run, it is people's support for conservation easements that makes easements effective vehicles for protecting land and historic resources. No matter how careful and conscientious your stewardship program is, it cannot assure the protection of resources in the face of property owners who are intent on violating them, public misunderstanding about or resentment against easements, or consistent lack of government support. Conversely, a stewardship program can be strengthened by conscientious and cooperative property owners, assistance by community members, and the help of local government. Strong property owner and community relations create a positive environment for sound stewardship.

Property Owner Contact

Cultivating a good working relationship with the property owner is fundamental to a successful stewardship program. A good relationship makes it less likely that the owner will violate the easement, and allows you to iron out the inevitable bumps and problems that arise in any easement over time. Use regular monitoring activities to build a spirit of cooperation with the property owner, and try to keep the owner informed about your activities and responsibilities regarding the easement property.

Before the Easement is Acquired

Review your stewardship responsibilities with the property owner during negotiations. This ensures the property owner is aware of what monitoring and enforcement will entail and understands up front that you are serious about your monitoring responsibilities. It gives the owner an opportunity to ask questions and participate in the monitoring planning, and imparts a sense of confidence that the easement will be cared for over time.

In such a meeting, explain the organization's legal right to inspect the property and enter it at reasonable times for monitoring purposes. Describe the monitoring procedure, including how and how often the organization will monitor, and show monitoring forms, photo procedures, and the like. Explain how documentation will be compiled and maintained. Discuss when the owner should expect to hear from the organization, and encourage the owner to accompany you on site inspections. Invite the owner to contact the organization with any questions about interpretation of the easement. If the property is leased, meet with the leaseholder too, or encourage the owner to pass along the information. Be sure the owner understands that anyone in his or her employment, or using the property under the owner's direct or indirect supervision, must abide by the conservation easement.

If you have written policies on monitoring and handling easement violations, it might be useful to share these with the property owner as well.

Owner Contact as Part of Monitoring

After acquisition, regular meetings with the property owner are as essential to effective stewardship as regular property inspections. They allow you to renew the cooperative relationship with the owner and review technical aspects of the easement. At a minimum you should meet with the property owner at least once every three to five years. You should also arrange a meeting whenever a problem or possible violation is detected or when the property has changed hands, even within the family.

If an owner lives far away, or if it is difficult to arrange a face-to-face meeting, you should periodically discuss the easement with the owner on the phone. Interacting with the owner, not just sending letters, is the best way to keep informed about the owner's plans and goals for the property.

MAINE COAST HERITAGE TRUST

Maine Coast Heritage Trust staff walk an easement property with the landowner. It's essential to explain monitoring and enforcement responsibilities early in negotiations, and to include the property owner in monitoring inspections if possible.

New Property Owners

Easement holders report that most easement violations are caused not by the original grantor, but by subsequent owners. New owners, who were not involved in easement negotiations, usually have little understanding of the restrictions. Meeting with the new owner and explaining the easement's terms will help prevent violations resulting from the new owner's ignorance, misinterpretation of the easement, or underestimation of your commitment to enforcing its terms.

Whenever the property changes hands, contact the new owner as soon as possible—or even better, before the property changes hands—to review the easement. In this contact—either by letter or in a meeting—take the following steps.

Introduce the organization and its goals. Explain how the easement and its restrictions fit with your organization's mission, its specific protection plans, and any other easements in the area.

Review the easement document, its restrictions, and your role in overseeing the restrictions. Explain how these restrictions were designed and what resources the easement was created to protect.

Discuss the monitoring policy, as outlined above.
In addition, you might want to take these actions:

Monitor the property, to document property condition at the start of the new ownership.

Ask the property owner to sign an acknowledgment of the easement. (See sample acknowledgement in Appendix H.)

Learning of Changes in Ownership

It's a good idea to include a provision in the easement requiring the owner to notify you when the property is transferred. Some easements also require the conservation easement to be referenced or incorporated in all subsequent deeds of transfer (see suggested language in the model easements in *The Conservation Easement Handbook*). However, property owners often overlook this requirement. Easement holders often learn of ownership changes through returned correspondence—which emphasizes the need to stay in regular written contact with the property owner. Some organizations inform local realtors about easement properties, and ask to be informed when a property is listed. Some easement holders periodically check local deed registries for transfer of their easement properties. You can also call the local tax assessor to check the current owner.

Be sure that every easement is properly recorded in the deed registry, so that a prospective owner's title search will pick it up. To help ensure that a prospective owner's title search will find an older easement, you can periodically record an inspection report or affidavit that acknowledges the easement. For example, if the title search standard is 42 years, you might re-record the easement every 40 years. The document should be signed by and include the names of the current property owner and the easement holder to insure that it will be properly indexed in the registry.

MONTANA LAND RELIANCE

Signs posted on protected property serve to educate the public about your organization and land protection program.

Community and Government Relations

You may call on neighbors, volunteers, other conservation and historic preservation organizations, and government officials to augment your stewardship program. Local people, who have more frequent day-to-day contact with the property than you, can be the best watchdogs for the easement. Some experienced easement holders say that the "nosy neighbor" is an important source of trespass and violation information. In addition, you can build a positive public image, strengthen your support in the community, find new supporters and members, and even bring new easements to the table by involving local people in your protection activities.

Building local interest and contacts begins with education. Provide information about conservation easements to increase public understanding of the restrictions on the property and win community support and cooperation for the easement program. But present the information with care—to protect the easement holder's and property owner's best interests. Make sure people understand how easements work and the purpose of each easement. Information that is incomplete or misunderstood may damage an easement program. You don't want people to think a scenic easement is a public park; it could lead to unintentional trespass on the property and a disappointed public, not to mention a disgruntled property owner.

A good way to build awareness of your easements—*if acceptable to the property owner*—is to publicize an easement acquisition by issuing a press release and holding an event to recognize the property's protection. For more permanent public visibility, some organizations use easement plaques or signs. Historic preservation easement holders often attach plaques to the facade or interior walls of protected structures. Each plaque includes the name of the easement holder and some reference to the existence of the protective easement. The plaque lets the public know that a property is protected and serves as an invitation to report violations to the easement-holding organization. Plaques or permanent signs strategically sited at the boundaries of protected open spaces could serve the same function. Be sure the easement does not prohibit erection of signs, or makes an exception for the identifying sign.

While informal contacts can be an important asset to your easement stewardship program, they are not a substitute for regular, documented monitoring carried out in accordance with the policies and under the supervision of your organization. You are the legal enforcer of the easement, and you cannot abdicate this responsibility to informal "watchdogs." In addition, such watchdogs may not appropriately represent your interests or develop the vital good relationship with the property owner.

Some types of community contacts that can be particularly helpful are described below.

Local Government

For private organizations holding easements, it is especially important to educate the local government about easement properties for several reasons:

- *An informed local government can help spot potential easement violations.* Local ordinances often require the owner to notify or obtain approval from the municipality for certain practices, such as subdivision, construction, timber cutting, or gravel mining. If a local board

JULIE MAYNARD, COURTESY MARYLAND ENVIRONMENTAL TRUST

This photo, published in a local paper, shows a land trust staff person with easement donors standing on a historic stone wall on their property. Such publicity photos and press events that recognize newly protected properties can help win the cooperation of the community.

is informed of easement restrictions, they may prevent activities that conflict with the restrictions, inform you before the owner embarks on such activities, or seek your approval for the requested activity.

- *An informed local government can include protected property in master planning.* Local and regional governments can include conservation properties on their maps and in their plans as they develop and revise master plans. An easement holder that doesn't inform local officials of its easements increases its odds of later fighting the municipality over planning, eminent domain, or land use regulatory issues.
- *Informing the local government is good public relations.* Just as you strive to build a cooperative partnership with the property owner, you should extend every effort to build a cooperative relationship with the community in which you work.

In exceptional situations, private easement holders sometimes choose not to inform the local government of an easement's existence. Certain property owners may require confidentiality as a condition of their gift. Or the organization may worry that, in the local political climate, the information will be misinterpreted, used against the owner, or otherwise abused.

Provide the following information to the local governing and planning bodies:

- name of owner
- date of gift
- tax map and parcel number
- number of acres under easement
- a statement summarizing the intent of the easement

The local government should be informed at the time the easement is acquired. Some organizations find it useful to send an annual reminder or update including a cumulative list of properties protected in that area. Since local jurisdictional bodies tend to turn over regularly, an annual reminder educates new government representatives about the easement.

Other government contacts

In addition to informing the local government and planning bodies, some easement holders provide the following entities with information about their easements:

- *Municipal boards.* This might include the conservation commission, zoning board of adjustment, architectural review board, or any other board empowered with making relevant regulatory decisions.

- *Local assessor or supervisor of assessments.* To the extent that local and state laws permit, the assessor should consider the easement restrictions in assessing the property. A fair tax record on easement properties encourages other owners to protect their property.

- *County and/or state planners.* Some states require all easements to be sent to county planners or to the state for comment prior to recording. Even if it's not required, regional planners appreciate knowing locations of easement properties.

- *Cooperative extension agencies.* Employees of agricultural and forest extension agencies, the Soil Conservation Service, and county conservation districts often appreciate knowing about easements. They may be able to assist owners in appropriate management of the restricted land. They also can provide outreach to other landowners who may be interested in protecting their land.
- *Local, regional, or state mapping agencies.* Inform agencies that keep maps of conservation land and property tax maps. Some use computer databases (Geographic Information Systems) to record mapped information. Getting the easement on the map makes a permanent, easily recognized, public record of the easement restriction. People who become aware of the easement may keep an eye on the property and inform the easement holder of potential problems. Supply mapping agencies with a survey, a property outline on a U.S. Geological Survey topographic map, or other relevant map to ensure accuracy of this record.

Neighboring Property Owners

You may want to send a letter explaining the easement to abutters and neighbors of the property. Do this both at the time of acquisition and from time to time thereafter. Invite their questions. Doing so may help deter them from violating the easement, and may gain their assistance in informally watching out for the easement. It may also generate their interest in easements for their own property.

Other Conservation and Preservation Organizations

Enlist the support of locally active conservation groups, volunteers, and interested citizens. Explain the purpose and the terms of the easement and the role of your organization, and invite questions and participation in informally watching over the property.

CHAPTER 6

Easement Enforcement: Dealing with Violations

An easement holder has a duty to take all reasonably necessary steps to rectify easement violations. In addition to protecting the conservation value of the property, enforcement is important for several reasons:

- *Strong enforcement engenders public confidence in the easement program.* Bill Sellers of the Brandywine Conservancy says, "We must not forget that we are not only defending one easement, we are defending all the easements we hold and every easement granted to every organization." Addressing violations proves to the owner and the public that you stand by your easements. By enforcing your easements, you discourage future violations and build a trustworthy reputation for your organization. You also help maintain the public's confidence in easements as a protection tool.

- *Enforcing the easement's terms helps maintain your legal authority to enforce.* Letting a violation slide could jeopardize your ability to enforce the easement. A court may interpret delayed enforcement as a waiver of the holder's right to enforce.

- *Egregious failure to enforce could jeopardize a private organization's capacity to accept tax-deductible easement gifts, as well as its tax-exempt status.* Treasury regulations specify that to be eligible to receive tax-deductible easement donations, an organization must "have a commitment to protect the conservation purposes of the donation, and have the resources to enforce the restrictions." (See Treas. Reg. § 1.170A-14(c)(1).) An organization's Section 501(c)(3) tax-exempt status also could be challenged if it were shown that the organization relinquished enforcement rights to the benefit of private individuals.

Being Prepared to Enforce

Even before you are faced with a violation, you should take steps to be sure you are prepared to deal with violations when they arise by developing a violations policy and by ensuring you have the financial resources to enforce. You should also be sure to include good enforcement language in the easement document. See the model easements in *The Conservation Easement Handbook* for suggested language.

Developing a Violation Policy

It is useful to develop written guidelines for responding to easement violations. Such a policy might address the following issues:

- How will the property owner be contacted, and who will have authority to discuss the violation with the owner?
- How will a violation be documented?
- In what circumstances and at what point will legal counsel be consulted?
- Who will have authority to negotiate a resolution with the property owner?

The demands of each violation are different and impossible to anticipate, but it helps to decide basic approaches before a violation puts pressure on you to act quickly. Thoughtful handling of a violation from the start can help position you favorably in subsequent negotiations with the property owner for reparation, or in future legal action if necessary. A sample violation policy is provided in Appendix I.

Ensuring Financial Resources to Enforce

You must have adequate financial resources to take action against violations. All easement documents should be drafted to include the right to recover all enforcement costs from the property owner in the event of a violation. (See *The Conservation Easement Handbook* for suggested language.) As a practical matter, however, it is sometimes impossible to recover costs, and even if the organization is later reimbursed for expenses, it will need to pay for many costs up front. You need to be sure you have or can raise the necessary funds. See Chapter 7 for a detailed discussion of potential stewardship costs and how to fund them.

Dealing with Violations

What Constitutes a Violation?

Only occasionally will an easement violation blatantly and unarguably conflict with the terms of an easement. More frequently, the situation is ambiguous. Sometimes undesirable activities are not clearly

JIM HIGHSAW, COURTESY MARYLAND ENVIRONMENTAL TRUST

JIM HIGHSAW, COURTESY MARYLAND ENVIRONMENTAL TRUST

Easement violations come in all sizes. Above, a barn constructed in violation of a conservation easement requiring prior written approval from the grantees for location, design, and appearance. Left, platform for an aerial ropes course constructed in violation of a conservation easement that prohibits structures and damage to trees and shrubs. Even small violations must be addressed.

addressed by the easement's terms. It is often necessary to interpret the terms of the easement and the effects of the undesirable activity in relation to those terms.

Sometimes interpretation of carefully crafted easements will yield conflicting results when confronted with a real-life situation. Take, for example, an easement on open farmland with a panoramic, 100-mile view sloping away from a public road. The easement is designed to protect both agricultural and scenic values. What if a new farmer plants an orchard, not specifically prohibited by the easement's terms, that will grow up to block the entire protected view? The easement holder must do its best to interpret the specific intent of the easement language. Such subjective interpretation is among the trickiest of an easement holder's responsibilities.

To determine whether a questionable activity is a violation of the easement, you should review the specific restrictions and stated conservation purposes of the easement. You should consult legal counsel or other experienced easement holders for assistance in interpreting the easement language. You could review the easement acquisition history for evidence of the intent of the grantor. You should also consult the baseline documentation and previous monitoring records to pinpoint when the activity or situation developed.

It makes sense to match the level of enforcement to the seriousness of the violation. Sometimes, you may choose to take only limited action against a minor technical violation of an easement, provided that the activity does not conflict with the overall purposes of the easement. For example, if a farm easement prohibits dumping but the farmer disposes of some organic, biodegradable waste deep in the woods, the disposal may technically violate the terms of the easement. However, if you judge that the activity is not inconsistent with the purposes of the easement, and it in no way appreciably impacts the conservation values of the property, you may limit your enforcement action to discussing the problem with the property owner so that he or she understands your concern. You should approach these sensitive violation identification issues with great care, since each decision you make may establish a precedent for the future.

Documenting the Violation

You may discover a violation on a monitoring visit, or through an abutter or other interested party, or during informal observation. The violation may have been caused by original owners, new owners, abutters, or trespassers. The owner may or may not be present when the violation is discovered. Whatever the circumstances, you should take two immediate steps: document the suspected violation and meet with the property owner to discuss the situation.

Document violations, like this illegal timber cut, with measurements, notes, and photos.

RICHARD OBER, COURTESY SOCIETY FOR THE PROTECTION OF NEW HAMPSHIRE FORESTS

A thorough and immediate record of the violation will be essential should you later need to go to court. Document the violation quantitatively and descriptively so that it can be assessed by an audience that does not know the property at all.

1. Take photographs, signed and dated by the photographer and keyed to the location where the photos were taken on a map; consider using a video camera with verbal commentary.

2. Measure the affected resource by whatever means are appropriate. If trees are cut in a restricted area, count the stumps and measure diameters, and take pictures of a ruler on the stumps. If an illegal road is bulldozed, map its position and record what was destroyed.

3. Take extensive field notes and sign and date them.

4. Compare and contrast the baseline documentation and relevant monitoring records to demonstrate the changed condition of the property.

Meeting with the Property Owner

Discuss the violation with the property owner right away. If the violation was discovered without the property owner present, contact the owner and arrange a meeting. A cooperative, face-to-face meeting to view the violation, review the easement restrictions, and discuss remediation is the most effective way to encourage the owner to take steps to correct the violation. If the violation is serious, whoever meets with the owner should be briefed by an attorney on proper procedures, conduct, correspondence, and other communication to be sure your legal interests are protected.

Dealing with third-party violations. If a third party caused the violation—dumping trash, for example—arrange another meeting to bring together all parties and discuss correction. If the third party violator is unknown or uncooperative, and if the violation is also a criminal trespass on the owner's property, it may be necessary to involve law enforcement officials to help bring the violator to the table. As much as possible, act constructively and cooperatively with the property owner when confronted with third party violations. Even if the owner did not cause the violation, be sure to include him or her in all negotiations. Legal responsibility for the violation usually falls on the property owner, depending on the exact easement language, but the third party violator should be held responsible for remediation to the extent possible.

Easement violations that violate the law. If the act prohibited by the easement violates any local, state, or federal laws—violations that alter wetlands or water courses, for example—you may need to notify law enforcement authorities as well. Consult legal counsel for advice on how to proceed.

Voluntary reparation. Try to negotiate voluntary restoration (or compensation if restoration is impractical) by the property owner or other party responsible for the violation.

Approaches to Enforcement

Voluntary Reparation by the Violator

A voluntary, negotiated resolution to a violation is the most common, and highly preferred, solution. Most easement violations are caused unintentionally by property owners, abutters, or other parties who were unaware of the easement, or who did not understand it or failed to take it seriously. Violators are often willing to make reparations that are negotiated with the easement holder. Voluntary remediation is the least costly and least antagonistic approach, and usually is the approach most likely to result in a full and timely repair of any damages. You should pursue this course until it is clear that it will be unavailing.

However, you should monitor this negotiation process carefully; the agreement could still break down. While face-to-face meetings are the best way to negotiate with the violator, a written record is essential. Carefully document the sequence and details of events as they happen. You should ask legal counsel to help plan a legally defensible strategy and program, depending on the type of violation and the attitude of the violator. Violations that damage an irreplaceable conservation value—for example, clearcutting a special forest habitat—will demand more than simply restoring the damage (such as by replanting trees). Legal counsel may be especially useful to develop and negotiate adequate reparation when complete restoration is impossible.

Some suggested steps to follow:

1. Take thorough notes to document all meetings. For example, write a memorandum to the violator summarizing each meeting, decision, and agreement.

2. Agree on a course of action to correct the violation.

3. Set an appropriate deadline for compliance. Make it clear that if compliance is not achieved by the deadline, a court case may ensue.

4. Write a letter to all parties to confirm the required restoration action and compliance deadline.

ROGER STERNBERG, COURTESY VERMONT LAND TRUST

Many easement violations, like this dump on a protected farm, can be adequately repaired if the easement holder takes prompt enforcement action.

5. When it is done, inspect and document the restoration work. Take extensive notes and photographs during property inspections of restoration work or subsequent violations. The record should be adequate to demonstrate the chain of events to a court, should litigation later become ncccssary.

Arbitration and Mediation

If the violator and easement holder cannot reach an agreement for remediation, but the violator is willing to cooperate with an outside party, arbitration or mediation may offer alternatives to the courtroom. The conservation easement terms may specify if and how arbitration and mediation may be used to solve disputes.

Easement Violation Case Study: Town of Rindge

The conservation commission for the Town of Rindge, New Hampshire, negotiated and accepted a conservation easement from a developer to protect the shoreline of a pond. The easement terms prohibited cutting any trees over two inches in diameter within a 25-foot setback from the edge of the pond. The subsequent owner, a builder, nevertheless clearcut a 60-foot strip of shoreline to provide a view to the pond.

The conservation commission discovered the violation by viewing the shoreline from across the pond. The commissioners tried, unsuccessfully, to arrange a meeting with the landowner. They then entered the property to document the violation, counting stumps and recording the diameters and species of trees cut. They informed the selectmen and town counsel, and the town attorney arranged a meeting with the builder and the property owner (who had subsequently purchased the affected lot from the builder).

The builder and new owner claimed to be unaware of the terms of the conservation easement (although it was referenced in the property deed), but the builder took responsibility for damages. The conservation commission designed a plan to restore, as much as possible, the damaged shoreline zone. The town required the builder to replace the 12 trees that were removed and to repair the disturbed bank. The work was required to be performed by a professional nurseryman. It also fined the builder $1,000, based on the estimate of how much value the lot had gained from the view of the pond. The builder agreed to the required reparations. The 12 trees were replaced and the bank seeded at his cost of $2,182. The builder also paid for the town attorney's time, $365. It took about five months from the time the violation was discovered to the time repairs were completed.

Easement Violation Case Study: Montana Land Reliance

The Montana Land Reliance, a private, nonprofit land trust, learned of a violation on one of its easements from the owner of the affected property. An adjacent landowner, a gravel company, had removed gravel, built a road, and disturbed a protected stream bed on the easement-encumbered property. The landowner contacted the gravel company and hired a surveyor to resolve the apparent misunderstanding of boundary locations. The landowner also thoroughly documented the violation with photos.

The landowner and the gravel company designed a plan for restoration, approved by the Montana Land Reliance, which the gravel company agreed to perform. The Montana Land Reliance also contacted its legal counsel, who advised the Reliance to continue meeting with both parties to resolve the situation, rather than bring in the threat of litigation. Six months later, when weather permitted, the gravel company repaired damages as much as possible, and the landowner and the Montana Land Reliance later inspected and approved the work.

This violation emphasizes the importance of clearly marking boundaries and notifying abutters of easement-protected land about restrictions.

In arbitration, the parties jointly hire, and pay for, an arbitrator (or arbitrators) who hears both sides and makes a decision. The decision is usually binding with no opportunity for appeal. Arbitrators are often, but not always, a quicker and less expensive solution than going to court. State laws may set rules for how and in what situations arbitration may be used. If you anticipate using arbitration, you may want to include provisions for it in the easement document (see *The Conservation Easement Handbook* for suggested language).

In mediation, the parties hire a mediator to assist them in negotiating a mutually agreeable solution. This gives the easement holder a role in negotiating an acceptable solution to the dispute.

You should carefully consider the merits of the case, and consult legal counsel, when choosing between arbitration or mediation and litigation. Arbitration and mediation may be less expensive and quicker, especially for relatively simple issues. But they both have disadvantages. With compromise or negotiation as their key features, arbitration or mediation may result in undesirable compromises that are counter to the easement's purposes. Arbitration usually cannot be appealed. No legal precedent is set, which may be an advantage or a disadvantage.

Litigation in some cases may be the preferred course. Some easement holders cannot use arbitration; federal and state agencies usually cannot agree to arbitration because it is perceived as an illegal delegation of authority. You may desire to seek a judicial interpretation of the respective rights of the easement holder and affected property owner. The court can provide a determination of appropriate damages, restoration, or mitigation for violations concerning hard-to-quantify values, like the destruction of endangered, threatened, or sensitive species. A court decision can set a valuable legal precedent in the event a similar situation arises in the future. In addition, only courts can issue an injunction to halt the offending activity.

Thomas Barrett, author of the Model Conservation Easement in *The Conservation Easement Handbook*, advises:

> Although arbitration has its virtues, it is no panacea. For relatively simple disputes involving questions that can be easily stated and that call for straightforward answers, arbitration may be appropriate. For more complicated matters, which could benefit from either the focusing that modern litigation, for all its faults, demands or the application of a court's plenary powers, arbitration can be a poor choice.

The Last Resort: Going to Court

Experienced easement holders consider going to court as a last resort. It is costly in time and money, it may irreversibly damage the relationship between the property owner and the easement holder, and a loss could set an unfavorable precedent that might affect easements in general.

You should go to court only if you believe in good faith that a substantial violation has occurred, that you can document the violation in court, and that the court is likely to interpret the activity as a violation of the easement. Get a careful analysis by an experienced trial lawyer. Because each case may have the potential to set precedent for future resolution of easement issues—perhaps even for every easement, nationwide—an organization should carefully consider the risks and ramifications of losing. Conversely, favorable resolution by a court of a critical legal issue or compensation for damages may be of great help to easement programs.

Sometimes easement holders must go to court. If a violator persists in prohibited activities that damage a protected resource, you must

Easement Violation Case Study: Forest Society of Maine

New England's largest conservation easement protects 18,000 acres in Attean Township, Maine, and is held by the Forest Society of Maine. A third party violated the easement by constructing several developed campsites on the easement-protected shore of Attean Pond. The campsites clearly violated the terms of the easement. The Forest Society of Maine worked with the landowner to document the violations and identify the violator.

The Forest Society of Maine inspected the site, documented the damages, and met with the violator. The violator did not voluntarily rectify damages, and caused further violations. The Society obtained a temporary restraining order from the court to halt further violations. The defendant defaulted on rectification of damages, and a permanent injunction and reparations were ordered by the court. The landowner then repaired the damages as much as possible. A motion for determination of monetary damages was filed by the landowner and the Forest Society, and the court ordered the violator to pay $18,000 to cover reparation costs and legal fees. The violator, as payment, deeded two building lots to the Society, which is currently marketing them.

seek a temporary restraining order or a preliminary injunction from the courts to stop it. Moreover, litigation may be the only course available to respond to a violator who refuses to voluntarily repair damages or cooperate with mediation or arbitration. Your bottom line must be to defend the easement.

If a violation requires court action, you should hire and thoroughly prepare the best legal counsel you can find. Actively participate in the formulation of the case. Use your documentation of the violation, baseline and monitoring documentation, and personal knowledge of the property to your fullest advantage. Be sure you have adequate enforcement funds to cover legal expenses.

For further guidance, land trusts should consult with a statewide land trust or regional organization of land trusts if there is one in your area. Determine whether your state attorney general is statutorily empowered or obligated to assist in defending the easement. Notify the Land Trust Alliance about major violations that might require litigation and/or set a national precedent. Since easements are still very young, few cases have been through the courts, and each case brought to litigation potentially affects all easement holders.

CHAPTER 7

Stewardship Funds

Every aspect of stewardship costs time and usually money, and the costs extend forever. And compared with raising funds for exciting new property protection initiatives, raising funds for ongoing stewardship is difficult. Nonetheless, as you protect more and more property, stewardship becomes a larger part of your budget. Every easement holder must recognize the costs of stewardship and decide how to meet them. Lack of financial planning will result in inadequate stewardship, failure to monitor and enforce, loss of easement conservation values, and loss of public confidence in conservation easements as a resource protection tool.

Estimating Stewardship Costs

An easement holder must plan to cover expenses of three types:

- baseline documentation development
- monitoring
- enforcement to correct violations

Costs vary depending on the complexity of easement provisions, the type of property, how monitoring is performed, availability of volunteer time, and the likelihood of violations.

Baseline Documentation and Monitoring Costs

The types of costs involved in doing the baseline documentation, and performing basic monitoring tasks, are similar. They include:

- *Time of staff, consultants, and/or volunteers.* Determine who will compile baseline data, perform routine monitoring tasks, visit the property and new owners as needed, maintain documentation, answer owner questions, and respond to violations. Estimate how much time these tasks will take, and what that time will cost.
- *Travel expenses.* Determine how much travel will be involved in compiling the baseline documentation and doing the monitoring, what type of transportation will be required, and what it will cost. For monitoring, estimate both the cost of getting to the property, and any transportation cost associated with monitoring by air or boat.
- *Maps and photos.* Determine the types of maps, plans, surveys, drawings, and photos needed for baseline documentation. What additional photos will be needed for monitoring? Consider, for example, costs of aerial photos and archival quality materials.
- *Administration.* Estimate costs of phone, mailing, photocopying, archival storage, and associated overhead costs. Preston Bristow, stewardship director of the Vermont Land Trust, which holds 25,000 acres under easement, notes, "Everyone trivializes the cost and time involved in administration and recordkeeping, but it is very real, especially in perpetuity."

Special Monitoring Costs

Certain easement provisions require special monitoring that can be the most expensive element of the stewardship budget. Easement holders that accept easements requiring approval for certain activities or technical monitoring capability must cover additional costs. For example:

- *Special monitoring provisions.* Determine how much it will cost to hire specialists needed to review and monitor particular easement provisions, such as water quality protection restrictions and architectural design review provisions.
- *Grantee approval provisions.* For easements with reserved building rights, consider the cost of staff or consultant time to review plans, hold conferences with the property owner, and do site inspections. Other easement provisions might require additional review time, such as approval of a woodland management plan.

Enforcement Costs

It is impossible to predict specific enforcement costs, but you need to have some working estimate. Costs might include:

- *Time.* The time involved in meeting and negotiating with the property owner and/or violator, documenting the violation and all subsequent action, and developing, reviewing, and inspecting remediation can be substantial. Consider who might handle this and what their time will cost.
- *Professional costs.* You may need a variety of technical services—architectural, engineering, boundary surveying, water quality testing, or timber surveying. You will also need legal counsel to review easement violations, advise on how to respond to violations, and potentially to defend the easement in court. Although the likelihood of going to court is relatively low, the potential expenses are large.

Establishing a Permanent Stewardship Fund

The surest way to meet stewardship costs is to set up a "Stewardship Fund" that is segregated from your operating budget. The goal is to have income from the fund (supplemented perhaps with principal in the case of an emergency) support most or all of your stewardship expenses. This fund helps ensure that monitoring and enforcement responsibilities will be met, even in lean times, and as your stewardship responsibilities grow.

Many private easement holders, especially larger, more established land trusts, already use such stewardship funds. However, small, unstaffed land trusts and local historic preservation organizations *especially* should try to set up stewardship funds, particularly to cover potential enforcement costs. All-volunteer organizations may rely on volunteer labor and the expertise of board members for monitoring. But when there is a serious violation, unstaffed organizations probably will have to hire professional services to do more of the work that a paid staff person would otherwise do. Likewise, smaller organizations are likely to have limited cash on hand. They particularly will need to plan to have liquid resources on which to draw for legal defense.

Public agencies that hold easements, especially those at the local level, may also benefit from setting up dedicated stewardship funds. Often public easement holders can rely on public employees, such as the town counsel, state attorney general, or municipal staff, or budget appropriations for easement monitoring and enforcement needs. However, these resources may be unavailable when needed most. And just as stewardship funds are among the most difficult for private groups to fundraise for, they are among the least popular line items in government budgets, and among the quickest to be cut in lean times. A dedicated stewardship fund, legally restricted in its use, can help address this problem.

Organizations that have seen their stewardship burden mount know the importance of a dedicated fund. "A stewardship endowment fund is a virtual necessity," says Darby Bradley, president of Vermont Land Trust. "To accept an easement without creating the fund is abdicating one's responsibilities to future trustees."

Financing the Stewardship Fund

To build a stewardship fund, you should try to "deposit" an appropriate amount to the fund each time you acquire an easement. Stewardship can be expensive: many private land trusts try to deposit amounts ranging from approximately $1,000 to $6,000 or $7,000 per easement (see further discussion below). For small or newly established organizations, it may be difficult to set aside the full amount needed to support stewardship costs for every easement. Nevertheless, you should aim to build a fund over time that can fully support your stewardship activities. Building the fund will not get any easier over time.

Donations from Grantors

The most common way for private land trusts to build their stewardship funds is to ask for a tax-deductible cash donation from the grantor of each easement. Such an approach initially may seem unreasonable. New easement holders often think, "How can we ask them for cash, when they're already giving up valuable property rights?" However, the property owner is usually the person who cares most about seeing the property protected in perpetuity, and making a donation to the easement holder's stewardship fund is the best way to assure that the easement can be effectively defended over time. Because stewardship money is particularly difficult to fundraise for, the burden especially falls on the property owner to help cover these costs.

Easement donors seek to see their property protected for future generations. They often are willing to make a contribution to the holder's stewardship endowment, to ensure the property will be cared for over time.

Most easement holders that request a donation ask that it accompany the easement grant. If this is impossible, some accept donations pledged over several years. On properties where the owner retains rights to create and sell house site parcels, some organizations defer stewardship fund contributions to coincide with the sale of the building sites. Some also accept donations other than cash, such as other land donated for resale or donation of services.

If you plan to request a stewardship fund donation from the property owner, *be sure* to discuss it early in the easement negotiations, usually at the very first meeting. Maine Coast Heritage Trust, which has negotiated numerous conservation easements, recommends making the request in person and handing out a policy statement to help pave the way. This helps avoid unpleasantly surprising or offending the property owner, and gives you a chance to explain your future costs and the calculation of the requested amount.

Many private easement holders are reluctant to accept conservation easements that are not accompanied by a contribution for stewardship. Vermont Land Trust, a statewide land trust, reports that it receives a contribution about 90 percent of the time. Brandywine Conservancy, a regional land trust in Pennsylvania, observes that "most landowners willingly provide an endowment once they understand the importance of the land trust being financially prepared to uphold the terms of their easement." Not every easement holder will find itself in such a favorable situation. You need to assess your own situation, but you should not underestimate the willingness of easement donors to help ensure that you are able maintain your promise to protect the property in perpetuity.

Fundraising

In some cases, the property owner is unwilling or unable to make a gift. You may be operating in an area where people have high value property but modest income. This is often the case with agricultural easements. In some areas, easements are not well established as a protection tool, and you may feel you will jeopardize your chance of obtaining any easement donations if you seek accompanying cash donations for stewardship as well.

In such circumstances, some easement holders regularly solicit monitoring funds from the community. Peconic Land Trust, on Long Island in New York, sets a target amount of cash contributions to be raised for an easement. If the donor does not make the contribution, the Trust attempts to raise it from the community with the help of the easement donor. You can look to neighboring property owners, conservation-minded members of the community, or perhaps the municipality for stewardship contributions. Government programs with easement acquisition budgets can sometimes set aside stewardship monies from their funds.

Internal Set-Asides

Because it can be difficult to fundraise specifically for stewardship, a few organizations that generally are unable to obtain donations from the property owners instead make an internal transfer of funds from their own annual operating income, or from the income of other established funds, to their stewardship fund. Some transfer a certain amount per easement. Some transfer any year-end surplus cash into the stewardship fund.

Calculating the Contribution

Because most easement holders that set aside funds for stewardship do so by requesting contributions from the property owner, this discussion focuses on how those contributions are calculated. The same principles can be applied by an easement holder that fundraises or sets aside its own funds.

What the Contribution Covers

Easement holders differ in the types of costs they try to have a contribution cover. Generating income for **annual monitoring** costs is usually the basis for calculating the size of the contribution.

Some easement holders, however, also include **baseline documentation** expenses in their contribution requests—Vermont Land Trust adds $600 to its request for this purpose. Others charge the property owner separately for baseline documentation or take it out of the general operating budget, since this is a one-time stewardship expense.

Organizations differ on how they handle **legal enforcement** costs. Some add a contribution to build enforcement funds. Brandywine Conservancy adds a minimum of $350 to each contribution calculation for this purpose. (The exact amount depends on an assessment of the legal risks of the particular easement and when legal problems might arise.) Other easement holders plan to fundraise separately for enforcement expenses, since they can run into the thousands of dollars and are extremely difficult to predict or estimate. The principal in the stewardship fund helps ensure that the easement holder will have funds available up front to cover enforcement costs. An easement holder should build some reserve to finance enforcement when necessary. Some organizations—generally those that rely on volunteers to do all monitoring—only have a "Legal Enforcement Fund"; some have two separate legal enforcement and monitoring funds.

Here are some methods used to calculate the stewardship fund contribution.

Flat amount, based on average costs per easement. Maine Coast Heritage Trust, a regional land trust, calculates that monitoring costs the Trust $175 per easement per year on average. The Trust requests a donation of $3,500 per easement which, at an interest rate of 5 percent, generates $175 per year. Income from the fund in excess of 5 percent is returned to the fund to keep the principal's value even with inflation.

The Vermont Housing and Conservation Board, a state-funded program that makes grants to state, municipal, and private groups to purchase property and easements, can also set aside funds for easement stewardship. Generally, it grants the applicant organization a flat $5,000 for stewardship per funded project, based on average estimated costs for stewardship.

This method is uncomplicated and straightforward. Of course, easements vary in their real stewardship costs, but the costs tend to average out over multiple easements. This method works best for an easement holder that accepts easements similar in acreage and complexity.

Amount based on acreage and complexity of restrictions. Vermont Land Trust estimates monitoring costs based on its past experience and two standard factors, acreage and number of reserved house sites. Estimating a 5 percent rate of return after adjustment for inflation, VLT sets the contribution request to generate adequate income to cover estimated costs.

Amount based on specific projected costs. Brandywine Conservancy calculates anticipated annual monitoring cost based on projected estimates of staff time for travel, in-house administration, property visits, special easement provisions requiring additional oversight (such as the number of reserved house sites), and direct costs. The donation requested generates this annual income at a 6 percent yield.

This fine-tuned method takes time, but probably best indicates the real costs of each easement. Factors to consider include the size and accessibility of the parcel, the types of adjacent land uses, and the terms of the restriction, including permitted uses and anticipated frequency of review and approval.

Amount based on percentage of value. Some easement holders base the suggested contribution on the value of the property. San Juan Preservation Trust in Washington State requests 1 percent of the assessed valuation of the property prior to the easement or $1,000, whichever is larger.

Amount based on property owner's ability to contribute. Most easement holders that finance stewardship primarily through donations by easement donors will waive or reduce the requested contribution if the property owner is unable to make a contribution. Conversely, some easement holders ask easement donors who have the ability to do so to consider contributing more toward stewardship than the amount normally requested, to help make up for easements for which stewardship was underfunded.

Easement holders are continually refining their methods for calculating the stewardship set-aside. As private easement holders have gained experience with easements, and have paid more attention to estimating their real monitoring and enforcement costs, they have tended to request larger stewardship contributions.

See Appendix J for sample contribution policies and calculations.

Managing a Stewardship Fund

Investment Policies

It is a good idea to pool stewardship monies into a single, separately accounted-for fund for easy administration and investment. Some easement holders create two separate funds: a stewardship endowment, from which only income is available for withdrawal; and a legal defense fund, from which principal is also available. This arrangement helps protect the stewardship principal from being depleted by a major enforcement expense. Remember that you have an obligation to donors of stewardship funds to actually use those funds for the purposes for which they were contributed, so that the stewardship fund should be accounted for as a separate, restricted fund. Stewardship funds actually may be pooled and invested with other funds for ease and higher return, as long as the fund's income and expenditures are accounted for separately.

Generally, your fund investment policy should emphasize protection of the principal and should promote growth of the fund to keep pace with inflation. Some easement holders plan to reinvest all or part of the annual income to build the fund. Some allocate end-of-year surplus, if any, or a percentage of each year's stewardship budget to build the fund. Others depend on increasing economies of scale, as they acquire new easements and spend less per easement, to keep the fund sufficient over time. The National Trust for Historic Preservation expects to earn approximately 8 percent annually on its stewardship fund, but plans to reinvest approximately 3 percent to prevent erosion of the principal by inflation. It makes contribution requests assuming only 5 percent of the income will be available for stewardship. Lakes Region Conservation Trust in New Hampshire works on the same principle, but operates with a more conservative policy, assuming a 7 percent interest rate and reinvesting 4 percent, leaving 3 percent of the income available for stewardship. Of course, these assumptions may be changed over time.

Fund Withdrawal Policies

Your governing body must set specific policies for when and under what circumstances withdrawals from the fund are allowed. You need to have separate policies for annual withdrawals for monitoring and emergency withdrawals for enforcement, if allowed. In setting such policies, you should evaluate the status of your stewardship fund in comparison with annual monitoring costs and set objectives. Are you more concerned with building the fund by returning income to it? Or are you more concerned with covering escalating annual monitoring costs that are a drain on your budget? In the early years of building a fund, and while monitoring costs are still relatively low, some organizations return all income to speed the building of the fund. Several other approaches are described here.

Withdrawals based on percentage of face value. Brandywine Conservancy withdraws 6 percent of the face value of its fund annually for its monitoring program. This creates a reliable income stream for the budget and preserves capital, but may or may not cover all monitoring program expenses. For the Conservancy, the 6 percent withdrawal does not currently cover all monitoring program expenses; it must be supplemented by other annual income.

Withdrawals based on specific costs. The Society for the Protection of New Hampshire Forests charges the fund for direct monitoring costs, such as aerial flight time, staff time, and photography. Because the Society monitors by air or with volunteers, monitoring costs are relatively low, and fund income exceeds direct costs. Generally, this method ensures that costs are covered, but may risk capital if costs exceed fund income.

Withdrawals based on income. Many private easement holders withdraw part or all of the annual income for general monitoring program expenses. Like withdrawal based on percentage of face value, this method guarantees income for the budget and preserves capital, but may or may not cover expenses. This method, however, allows an organization easily to set and achieve specific growth goals for the fund. For example, some organizations reinvest 3 to 5 percent of the income as a hedge against inflation and only withdraw income over that level.

Withdrawals for enforcement. Many easement holders expect to invade fund principal for major enforcement expenses, such as legal defense. If you follow such a policy, you will need to plan to reimburse the fund for any significant amount of principal that is withdrawn for enforcement. Some costs may be recovered from the violator, if the easement so stipulates, but the easement holder could lose the case and not be eligible for reimbursement, or may be unable to recover all of its costs. Organizations that plan to withdraw principal from stewardship funds may well need to fundraise to replenish it.

A few easement holders view the fund principal as a true endowment, which can never be touched. They use the interest to cover annual monitoring costs and plan to raise enforcement funds elsewhere when the need arises.

CHAPTER 8

Long-Term Stewardship Issues: Back-Ups, Condemnation, Amendments

This chapter briefly touches on three additional issues related to long-term management of conservation easements. For further information, refer to *The Conservation Easement Handbook.*

Back-Ups: A Second Line of Defense

To provide the best assurance that its conservation easements will continue to be protected, an easement holder should consider making arrangements to have its easements monitored and enforced in the event it goes go out of business or otherwise is unable to meet its stewardship responsibilities. For new land trusts just getting started, easement donors frequently seek such assurance before giving easements.

A range of options exist. At a minimum, the easement should specify that it will be transferred to another qualified organization if the holder is dissolved. The easement may specify a back-up holder. Or it may be held by more than one organization at the same time, each with the independent ability to monitor and enforce the easement.

The options are limited by state law. Some states have specific statutory provisions; others do not and common law rules apply. The options also will vary depending on the availability of back-up organizations in the area and the type of organization involved. For example, an easement holder cannot be expected to plan back-up protection if there is no other appropriate and willing easement holder. And established, experienced, and well-funded easement holders may not think it useful to ask a less stable organization to play a back-up role. In any case, if an easement holder finds it no longer wants or is able to meet its easement stewardship responsibilities, it must find a way to ensure ongoing protection of its easements. Where no other organization is willing or able to step in, the attorney general of the state where the property is located usually has authority to assure that the easement is enforced.

IRS Requirement: Transfer Upon Dissolution

At a minimum, IRS regulations require that every tax-deductible easement must include a provision that allows the easement holder to transfer the easement to another entity only if the transferee is a "qualified organization" and agrees to enforce the easement's restrictions. This provision should be included in all easement documents, in case the organization dissolves or cannot uphold its stewardship responsibilities in the future. See *The Conservation Easement Handbook* for sample easement language for this provision.

Back-Up by Named Third Parties

Easement holders use several different back-up mechanisms that give a named third party certain rights to intervene in the easement's enforcement under certain circumstances. Keep in mind that state law may limit who can enforce an easement and serve as a back-up. A few examples of back-up arrangements are given here:

- The easement identifies a specific organization to whom the easement is transferred if the primary holder ceases to exist or to be a qualified organization under Section 170(h) of the Internal Revenue Code. Some organizations call this type of back-up organization a preferred transferee.
- The easement gives another organization the power to terminate the primary holder's interest in the easement if it fails to enforce the easement's terms. Some provisions allow the back-up organization to take title to the easement simply by recording notice in the deed registry; others require that a court must first approve the substitution, after finding that the primary easement holder has failed in its duties. This is often called an executory interest.
- The easement gives another organization the power to enforce the easement with the primary holder or alone if the primary grantee

fails to enforce. However, the easement title remains with the primary easement holder. This is commonly called a third party right of enforcement.

- In the case of easements acquired by one organization but transferred for long-term stewardship to another, the easement may provide that title reverts to the original grantee if the easement holder fails to enforce its terms.

Regardless of the type of arrangement, the primary holder should secure the agreement of any back-up interest it wishes to include in the easement. It is a good idea to include the potential back-up organization in the easement negotiations with the property owner, to make sure the easement terms will be acceptable. The back-up organization only adds protection if it is willing to take on the responsibility.

Back-ups that have enforcement rights have an additional level of involvement in the easement's stewardship. The primary holder should keep such back-ups informed about the status of the easement. Provide the back-up organization with documentation relevant to the easement, including baseline documentation and evidence of routine monitoring, so that the back-up will be prepared to act if necessary. Correspondingly, the back-up should check with the primary organization regularly, to make sure the easement is being monitored and enforced.

The back-up organization must plan for its stewardship costs. If an easement is transferred to a back-up, any stewardship fund donation that accompanied the easement should also be transferred to the back-up. If the back-up organization has back-up enforcement rights, it must plan to cover its annual costs of checking with the primary holder to be sure it is monitoring and enforcing the easement. The Society for the Protection of New Hampshire Forests, which does such a check annually, estimates this level of stewardship costs the Society about one-third the cost of full stewardship, on average, and requests contributions to its stewardship fund based on that cost.

Co-Holding

Another way to help ensure the enforcement and longevity of an easement is for two or more organizations to jointly hold (co-hold) the easement. Co-holding can also bring together different strengths or abilities to easement stewardship. Maryland Environmental Trust (MET), for example, a government-funded statewide land trust, co-holds easements in the state with local land trusts and the Maryland Historical

Trust, a state agency, providing added credibility, security, and certain tax advantages available only to easements held by MET. The Lancaster Farmland Trust and the Lancaster County Conservancy co-hold easements in which both farmland and natural resource values are involved, which takes advantage of the expertise of each organization. A potential disadvantage may be disagreements among easement co-holders and confusion on the part of the landowner.

Organizations joining as easement co-holders may share stewardship responsibilities equally, or they may individually accept primary responsibility for different elements of stewardship. Whatever the arrangement, the co-holders should delineate their roles at the time of acquisition, to avoid later conflict. For example, The Trustees of Reservations, a statewide land trust in Massachusetts that co-holds several easements with local land trusts, sets forth the basic relationship in the easement document and uses a memorandum of understanding to define the details. Details to consider include: Who is responsible for monitoring? Who has enforcement authority? Who reviews and approves any reserved rights requiring approval by the easement holder? Who decides on amendment proposals?

Each co-holder must keep the other informed about the status of its share of stewardship responsibilities. Each co-holder must also plan for its share of stewardship costs.

No state conservation easement statute provides for co-holding. These statutes provide for only one holder. Co-holding should be undertaken with care and only after approval by your attorney.

Condemnation of Easements

If property is needed for a public purpose such as a school, road, or sewage treatment plant, it may be taken by a government agency, even against the wishes of the private owner. If the property is restricted by a conservation easement that prevents the proposed use, the restrictions may also be terminated by condemnation. All easement holders except the federal government are potentially subject to condemnation: state easements may be condemned by federal action; local government easements by the state or federal governments; and private easements by government agencies at all levels. Some easement holders are concerned that a block or corridor of open space protected by easements may, in fact, be seen as an attractive and relatively inexpensive place to locate such public facilities and will be at a higher risk for public taking.

Easement properties may be condemned for a variety of public purposes, including pipeline rights-of-way. When faced with a potential condemnation, easement holders should consult legal counsel to ensure their legal and financial interests are fully protected.

Easement holders have faced condemnation situations. One land trust had a portion of an easement-protected marsh threatened with condemnation for a rest area along a public highway. One had several easement-encumbered properties threatened with condemnation by a gas pipeline. (Both of these were settled out of court. The latter is described in "When Condemnation Threatens Conservation Easements," *Exchange: The Journal of the Land Trust Alliance*, Vol. 8, No. 2, Spring 1989, which discusses a number of the issues involved in condemnation.)

Easement holders faced with a potential condemnation of the easement's restrictions face a number of difficult issues. Should the easement holder defend against the taking? What should be its role with the property owner in making that decision, and what should be their relative roles in fighting the condemnation if they decide to do so? If defeating the condemnation is impossible or undesirable, should the easement holder negotiate a voluntary settlement? Again, what should the respective roles of the property owner and easement holder be? How should negotiated compensation be allocated among these interests?

David Shields of Brandywine Conservancy in Pennsylvania, which has experienced several condemnation situations, emphasizes the importance of having an easement document that allows settlement out of court. The easement holder, property owner, and condemning agency can then enter a negotiated settlement process that can examine the conservation and financial value of the interests being condemned, and design a way to proceed with the least amount of damage.

In the event that a settlement is not reached voluntarily and the government condemns the property, the law clearly specifies that the property owner must be compensated for rights taken. The nature and extent of compensation to the easement holder, however, is a complex legal issue and may vary from state to state. Easement holders faced with a potential condemnation should consult experienced legal counsel to ensure that their legal and financial interests are fully protected.

Amending Easements

As easements mature, it is likely that property owners will seek amendments to modify the terms of the easement. Some amendments may have no practical effect on the conservation values, or may even be advantageous. Sometimes easement holders want to improve the easement with amendments to clarify vague language, correct oversights or errors in the original document, allow an unanticipated but acceptable use, or add new provisions to strengthen the easement. Sometimes the impact will be ambiguous or negative.

Easement holders must approach amendments with great care. They involve complex legal issues. And the question of when it is acceptable to amend an easement is just beginning to be explored. Abuse of amending easements will undermine the public credibility of the land trust and could raise charges as serious as tax fraud. Each potential amendment must be thoughtfully examined and decided.

Legal Issues

Approach amendments only with experienced legal advice. "In almost every jurisdiction, the laws that apply to amendment of conservation easements are conflicting or unsettled," observes Karin Marchetti Warden, general counsel for Maine Coast Heritage Trust. State law regarding conservation easements, charitable trust law, contract law, nonprofit corporation law, public trust law, and the IRS all might have something to say about if and how amendments are permitted.

Amendment Policy

It's wise to develop an amendment policy rather than making case-by-case responses to requests. An amendment policy can set clear rules for when and why amendments may be allowed. Also, an established policy will help you be consistent and fair when dealing with emotionally charged property owners making amendment requests. Preston Bristow of Vermont Land Trust, which has a written amendment policy, says that most of their amendment requests end once the owner reads the policy.

When developing an amendment policy, you must consider the laws of your state. You also should determine by what procedure amendment requests will be handled. Who will be consulted, and who will decide? What property factors must be considered (for example, net effect of the amendment on conservation value and financial value of the land)? Among easement holders that have developed amendment policies, it is widely viewed that the net effect of any amendment must strengthen or be neutral to the easement, and that the amendment must not result in a net increase to the owner's property value.

See Appendix K for a sample amendment policy. Consult the Land Trust Alliance or *The Conservation Easement Handbook* for further information.

Appendices: Special Note

The sample policies, forms, and documents provided in these appendices are provided as examples, not models. Each easement holder must evaluate its own circumstances, including relevant state law, and develop policies and forms appropriate to its needs. The Land Trust Alliance has supplemental packets of policies and forms available on many of these topics. Contact LTA for more information.

APPENDIX A

Basic Rules for Recordkeeping

Thoughtful and detailed recordkeeping, and safe storage of those records, is essential to a sound easement stewardship program. Recordkeeping occurs at several stages of stewardship: baseline documentation, monitoring, enforcement, and at various decisionmaking stages. Key principles about recordkeeping are summarized here.

Key records to keep include the following:

- Full baseline documentation file.
- Monitoring records, including correspondence with the property owner, photos, maps.
- Final documentation of action on property owner requests for approval to exercise reserved rights.
- Final documentation of exercised reserved rights.
- Documentation of violations and their resolution.
- Documentation of action on amendment requests.
- Documentation relating to the interpretation of any of the easement's terms.

In keeping these records, consider these recommendations.

Use archival quality materials. It is important to use materials that help ensure your records will last. Some easement holders recommend using acid-free paper and archival quality storage sleeves for photos. Opinions differ as to whether negatives, prints, or slides are most stable, but proper storage in a cool, dry place is essential regardless. Archival quality processing is available for some types of film.

Store records in a safe place. Store original records in a safe, fireproof location, such as a bank safe deposit box or fireproof file. If videotapes are used, protect them from magnetic or electrical disturbance. Be sure key people in the organization know where the records are stored and can get access to them if necessary.

Use standard forms tailored for your needs. Design and use standard forms for routine stewardship needs, such as baseline documentation checklists, easement summaries, and monitoring inspection forms. These will help ensure that all the necessary data are collected, and that future stewards can interpret the records and continue to collect consistent data.

Sign and date photos, notes, and recordkeeping forms. Besides helping your successors get back to the source if they have questions about an easement file, this also helps establish the file as legally admissible evidence.

If you have many easements, consider using a computer database. A few organizations with many easements have begun to keep some of their records, such as property information and monitoring history, on a computerized database. As an organization accumulates easements, the database may become increasingly useful to track the regular monitoring schedule and flag easements that need special attention.

Provide for continuity. The file for each easement should be sufficiently self-explanatory so that a new steward can understand the easement's terms, history of acquisition and monitoring, and any enforcement actions or property owner issues, and thus take up stewardship activities wherever they were left off. Every individual who adds records to an easement file should keep future stewards in mind. Records need to be sufficiently explicit and thorough to make sense to the steward in charge 20 years from now.

Keep records that can stand up in court. Your records must be sufficient to provide the basis for defending an easement in court. Since few easements have gone to court, there is little experience from which to define minimum legal standards for recordkeeping. Clearly, however, too much recordkeeping is better than too little.

Easement holders that have litigated easement violations observe that clear recordkeeping, good photos, and excellent baseline documentation made their day in court much easier.

Thorough records help establish who caused a violation, when it occurred, and what damage it caused. Good records place you in a sound position for negotiating with the violator for reparation. They also prove to the court and the public that you are doing your job.

It is a good idea to go over the requirements of admissible evidence in your jurisdiction with a knowledgeable attorney, to make sure your recordkeeping will be adequate for use in court. If a serious violation occurs, consult a lawyer to make sure your legal interests are covered and proper records of enforcement actions are kept.

It is never too late to upgrade recordkeeping, even for older easement files. As easement holders learn through experience, they often add written information or photos to old, inadequate files, while setting higher standards for new stewardship records.

APPENDIX B
IRS Baseline Documentation Regulations

Treasury Regulation Section 1.170A-14(g)(5)(i)

(5) Protection of conservation purpose where taxpayer reserves certain rights. (i) Documentation. In the case of donation made after February 13, 1986, of any qualified real property interest when the donor reserves rights the exercise of which may impair the conservation interests associated with the property, for a deduction to be allowable under this section the donor must make available to the donee, prior to the time the donation is made, documentation sufficient to establish the condition of the property at the time of the gift. Such documentation is designed to protect the conservation interests associated with the property, which although protected in perpetuity by the easement, could be adversely affected by the exercise of the reserved rights. Such documentation may include:

(A) The appropriate survey maps from the United States Geological Survey, showing the property line and other contiguous or nearby protected areas;

(B) A map of the area drawn to scale showing all existing man-made improvements or incursions (such as roads, buildings, fences, or gravel pits), vegetation and identification of flora and fauna (including, for example, rare species locations, animal breeding and roosting areas, and migration routes), land use history (including present uses and recent past disturbances), and distinct natural features (such as large trees and aquatic areas);

(C) An aerial photograph of the property at an appropriate scale taken as close as possible to the date the donation is made; and

(D) On-site photographs taken at appropriate locations on the property. If the terms of the donation contain restrictions with regard to a particular natural resource to be protected, such as water quality or air quality, the condition of the resource at or near the time of the gift must be established. The documentation, including the maps and photographs, must be accompanied by a statement signed by the donor and a representative of the donee clearly referencing the documentation and in substance saying "This natural resource inventory is an accurate representation of [the protected property] at the time of the transfer."

APPENDIX C

Sample Easement Summary Form

CONSERVATION EASEMENT ABSTRACT

(from the Society for the Protection of New Hampshire Forests)

GRANTOR/NAME OF PROPERTY:____________________________

Current Owner:__________________________Phone: ____________

Address:____

____

Easement Size (acres):_______Location:____________________

Registry Recording Information: Book_________Page__Date_________

BACK-UP ORGANIZATION (if applicable):

Name:_______________________________Phone: ____________

Address:____

____

PURPOSE OF EASEMENT (why the property was protected):

RESTRICTIONS (note any restrictions unique to this property):

RESERVED RIGHTS OR SPECIAL CONDITIONS (note when any reserved rights are exercised):

ATTACHMENTS:

___Topo Map With Property Bounds Drawn In

___Survey Plan

___Photos (aerial or ground)

___Monitoring Inspection Record

APPENDIX D

Sample Baseline Documentation Checklist

EASEMENT DOCUMENTATION REPORT CHECKLIST

(from The Nature Conservancy)

INTRODUCTION: All items below must be provided on the Documentation Report. The volume and specificity of information required by this checklist will vary depending on the terms of the easement. The intent of this format is to allow flexibility in the documentation technique and to key the quantity and nature of the documentation to the terms of the easement. Some conservation easements may require very general descriptions of plan cover, geology, soils, etc. Other descriptions may need to be narrower in scope and more detailed to ensure adequate monitoring of specific element occurrences. The legal and biological monitoring functions may overlap to some extent.

CHECKLIST:

____Cover Page

____Checklist

____Owner Acknowledgment of Condition (standard form letter must be notarized and should list all topics included in the documentation package)

____Background Information (brief, narrative history of easement acquisition: summary of current status; location of/directions to property)

____Legal Information (list of restrictions and retained rights, easement recordation data, name of benefitted preserve if applicable)

____Ecological Features (narrative description keyed to restrictions and retained rights: can include target element occurrences, other plant cover types, other wildlife, geology and soils, aquatic resources)

____Land Use and Man-Made Features (narrative description of improvement, structures, trails, wells, power lines, pipelines, etc., include historic use if appropriate)

____Photographs (aerial photo [recommended]; on-site photos should be keyed to restrictions and retained rights)

  ____aerial

  ____on-site

____Maps

  ____location of property: 1) state map showing property location; 2) 8 1/2" x 11" section of local road map showing property location; 3) 8 1/2" x 11" or larger topo map section showing property boundary

  ____ecological and man-made features as needed (can be mapped on topo map above or on separate maps to ensure clarity and adequacy of documentation; can include target element occurrence locations, structures/buildings, other plant cover types, trails, geology and soils, wells, aquatic resources)

BE SURE TO DATE AND HAVE PHOTOGRAPHER/PREPARER SIGN ALL PHOTOS, MAPS, ILLUSTRATIONS, ETC. ALSO PROVIDE A DESCRIPTION OR MAP SHOWING WHERE ON-SITE PHOTOS AND ILLUSTRATIONS WERE TAKEN (FOR ORIENTATION/COMPARISON PURPOSES).

APPENDIX E

Sample Baseline Documentation Form

BASELINE DOCUMENTATION INVENTORY

(from the Iowa Natural Heritage Foundation)

I. Introduction

A. Location
1. property name, county, state
2. legal description
3. property size (acres & hectares)
4. name of quad map, series, coordinates of property

B. Purpose for preservation
1. critical elements to be protected
2. other reasons (habitat preservation, unique or unusual ecological features, etc.)

C. How conservation easement will preserve critical elements (be brief). Examples include: by prevention of subdivision, house building, off-road vehicular travel, access control, controlled hunting, etc.)

D. Study methods here or in Appendix

Graphics

- General location map, locate property on county road map. In text.
- Topographic contour lines and property lines on 1" = 1000' USGS maps, in Appendix.
- Property base map with property boundary lines on 1" = 660' base map in Appendix.

II. Natural Resources of the Property

A. Use black and white photographs liberally to illustrate inventory features. Locate point and direction of photograph on property base map (picture point) and record date, time of day and weather conditions. Use of color photographs is unacceptable as many will fade over time.

B. Physiographic and ecological setting of the property
1. Locate property physiographically (i.e., West of Mississippi River in driftless region)
2. Location of property in the context of applicable land form regions of Iowa (See Iowa Geological Survey)
    a. Focus property further in the context of critical elements to be protected (e.g., Critical area to be protected under Protected Water Area General Plan)

C. Geology & Soils
1. Geology
    a. Stratigraphic units - bedrock & surficial deposits

APPENDIX E

(Continued)

b. Structure (faults, folds, etc.)
c. Present geomorphic processes
d. Geologic hazards
e. Minerals, oil and gas and requisite ownership

2. Soils
   a. Description of major soil units - SCS classifications
   b. Discussion of the unique aspects of and major limiting characteristics of each soil type (unique aspects that may affect habitat types, erodibilty, fragility, irrigability, etc.)

Graphics

- If important, map surficial geology on 1" = 660' base map. In text.
- Map mineral (coal, oil and gas, etc.) ownership if there is more than one owner. In Appendix.
- If important, map soils on property base map. In text.

D. Climate (if appropriate)

E. Hydrology (if appropriate)
1. Surface hydrology
   a. water quality
      1) abiotic - visual estimations of the geomorphic characteristics
      2) biotic - survey of aquatic flora or fauna as indicator of long-term aquatic quality indicators (such as streambank vegetation presence or absence as an indicator of turbidity problems).
   b. special classifications or descriptions (perennial stream, bog, fen, cold spring, etc.)
   c. meandered or non-meandered streams or lakes
2. Subsurface hydrology

F. Vegetation
1. Habitat types (floodplain timber, prairie, wetland, etc.)
   a. potential
   b. present condition
2. Rare plants

Graphics

- Map of habitat types and rare plants on 1" = 660' base maps. In text.

G. Wildlife
1. Important species, list and explain importance
   a. mammals (if appropriate)
   b. amphibians (if appropriate)
   c. birds (if appropriate)
   d. reptiles (if appropriate)
   e. fish (if appropriate)
   f. invertebrates (if appropriate)

Graphics

- Map wildlife habitat on 1" = 660' base map (if applicable). In text.

III. Baseline Description of Critical Elements

A. Demographics of critical element property (occurrence and population size).

B. Specific reference(s).

Graphics

- Map critical element occurrence if applicable on 1" = 660' base map. In text.

IV. Historic Land Use

(The conservation easement probably will restrict land use practices of the grantor. It is therefore very important that all land use practices, past, present and allowed under the terms of the conservation easement, be accurately recorded in the baseline report.)

A. Describe as accurately as is practical past land use and its effects on any of the natural resources of the property.

B. Describe present land use and the effect on any of the natural resources of the property.

C. List all important man-made structures and/or improvements on the property. Include information and location of any known archaeological sites.

V. Existing Land Use Plans

Reference appropriate federal, state, local or private plans or studies that identify specific uses or needs for the property.

Graphics

- Map and photograph all man-made structures and/or improvements on a 1" = 660' base map (e.g., buildings, fences, powerlines, irrigation ditches, roads, ponds, etc). In text.

APPENDIX FOR BASELINE REPORTS

1. Original USGS quadrangle with property lines and topographic contours, scale 1" = 1000'.
2. Property base map with property lines, scale 1" = 660'. Superimpose picture points.
3. Aerial photograph with property lines.
4. Plant list (if plant species diversity is not the primary concern of this conservation easement, a complete species list is unnecessary). (Reference who did it and when.)
5. Fauna list (if animal species diversity is not the primary concern of this conservation easement, a complete species list is unnecessary).
6. Original methods and inventory sheets.

APPENDIX F
Sample Monitoring Form

EASEMENT MONITORING INSPECTION REPORT
(from the Trust for New Hampshire Lands)

19__

1. Easement Name:
   Location:

   Current Owner:
   Address and Phone:

   Local contact for owner (as necessary):
   Address and Phone:

2. **Description of Current Land Use:**

3. **List Man-Made Alterations** (for example, construction, dredging or filling, new trails, timber harvest, clearing of new fields) since the easement was last monitored. Please describe activity or alteration; note location, extent, purpose, individual responsible (if known). Attach maps, photos, illustrations.

4. **List Natural Alterations** (for example, flooding, fire, insect infestation). Note location and nature of changes. Attach maps, photos, illustrations as necessary.

5. To the best of your knowledge and observation, are restrictions in the conservation easement being complied with? Please describe.

6. Other observations/comments.

METHOD OF INSPECTION: Ground / Air (circle one)

DATE OF INSPECTION:

LIST ALL PERSONS ATTENDING INSPECTION (landowner or others):

MONITOR'S NAME:

SIGNATURE:

ADDRESS AND PHONE:

PLEASE INDICATE THE NUMBER OF THE FOLLOWING ATTACHED TO THIS REPORT. BE SURE TO DATE AND SIGN ALL MATERIALS AND PROVIDE A DESCRIPTION OR MAP SHOWING WHERE ON-SITE PHOTOS AND ILLUSTRATIONS WERE TAKEN:

____aerial photo
____ground photos
____maps
____illustrations
____other:____

APPENDIX G

Sample Reserved Rights Approval Form

REQUEST FOR APPROVAL
(from the Sonoma Land Trust)

Prepared by:	**Date:**
Landowner Information	**Project ID**
Name:	Name:
Address:	AP#:
	Location:
Telephone:	

Action Requested for Approval:

Relevant Easement Provisions: (Easement Summary attached)

Does request provide sufficient information upon which to base action? ______

Are any federal, state or local permits required? (List)

Date request for approval received: ________Date of site visit:______

Findings by after Document Review & Site Visit:

Recommendation to Board: [ ] Approve [ ] Deny
Date:

Board Action Taken: [ ] Approve [ ] Deny
Date:

Conditions:

APPENDIX H

Sample Owner Acknowledgment

ACKNOWLEDGMENT
OF
GRANT OF EASEMENT
AND
DECLARATION OF RESTRICTIVE COVENANTS

(from the Brandywine Conservancy)

(Buyer) has entered into an agreement to purchase the (Seller) property. [Identify by name, if appropriate, and by title and deed number or tax number.]

Approximately (#) acres of the property are subject to land use restrictions contained in a Grant Of Easement And Declaration Of Restrictive Covenants (Grant of Easement), dated (date of signing), between the Brandywine Conservancy, Inc., and (Donor/Seller).

The Brandywine Conservancy, Inc., holds the Grant of Easement exclusively for conservation purposes and is responsible for administering, monitoring, and enforcing the terms and conditions therein.

Buyer hereby acknowledges the following:

1. Buyer has received a copy of the Grant of Easement;
2. Buyer has read the Grant of Easement prior to settlement;
3. Buyer understands and acknowledges the terms and conditions of the Grant of Easement;
4. Buyer understands that, as purchaser of the (Seller) property, Buyer is obliged to comply with all of the terms and conditions of such Grant of Easement;
5. Buyer understands that certain uses of and activities on the (Seller) property require prior approval from the Conservancy and that other uses and activities are prohibited; and
6. Buyer agrees to abide by the terms and conditions of the Grant of Easement.

ACKNOWLEDGED:

____
(Buyer) Date

APPENDIX I

Sample Violation Policy

CONSERVATION EASEMENT VIOLATION POLICY

(from the Brandywine Conservancy)

I. Violation Prevention

A. To improve easement compliance, it is suggested that the listing brokers of eased propertiese be contacted and informed about easements in general and the specific limitations of the subject easement. We should also insist that all buyers of eased land meet with a Conservancy staff member prior to settlement so that we may explain the easement.

B. It is suggested that we sponsor a general meeting with area real estate brokers (or those who often deal with easement properties) to explain easements and the Conservancy's policy for monitoring and enforcement.

II. Source of Violation Notification

A. Summer interns

B. Random staff observation

C. Third party informants (i.e., neighbors)

D. Easement donors

E. Townships, banks, title companies

III. Types of Violations

A. Minor: e.g., roadside trash, minor tree cutting

B. Major: e.g., construction, excavation, pollution, timbering

1. after the fact/irreversible; requires compensation and/or reclamation
2. on-going; requires cease/desist and restore order
3. before the fact/reversible; requires review and analysis

C. Common Violations

1. dumping
2. tree cutting
3. construction without Conservancy approval
4. property sale without notice
5. draining of wet areas

(continued next page)

IV. Violation Response Policy

A. Report and describe violation to designated staff member.

B. Review easement document.

C. Visit site, physically inspect violation.

D. Evaluate violation and required corrections.

E. Contact violator by telephone. Explain problem and Conservancy policy; request correction, replacement and/or cessation of activity; state deadline for compliance (e.g., immediately, 7, 14, 21, or 30 days.) BE COURTEOUS.

F. Follow up phone call with letter. Reiterate oral explanations and requests (e.g., why it's a violation, corrective measures required, deadline for compliance), offer of assistance; need for compliance inspection.

G. Inspect site at deadline date.

H. If prompt compliance, send thank-you note.

I. If non-compliance, send second letter. Be firm; cite Conservancy vested interests; restate required corrections, establish new shorter deadline date; copy to Conservancy attorney.

J. Inspect site at second deadline date.

K. If prompt compliance, send thank you note.

L. If non-compliance, notify EMC Director or Assistant Director. Determine new response. Send third letter. Give notice of impending legal action if immediate compliance not achieved. Copy to attorney.

M. Call attorney to discuss legal action. Have attorney send letter requesting compliance.

N. Initiate Conservancy corrective measures (optional).

APPENDIX J
Sample Stewardship Fund Policies

THE STEWARDSHIP FUND: AN ENDOWMENT FOR MONITORING, MANAGEMENT, & ENFORCEMENT

(from the Lakes Region Conservation Trust)

After the Lakes Region Conservation Trust accepts a conservation easement, its protection of the land has only just begun. From then on, in perpetuity, the Trust has the legal obligation to monitor regularly the use of the land and to enforce the restrictions of the easement when they are violated, tasks that can be costly.

To carry out the Trust's stewardship role, staff or trained volunteers visit the land at least once each year, either by foot or plane, to determine the consistency of the use of the land with the easement's restrictions. The monitor prepares a report and sends a letter to the landowner with the findings. If a violation is found, the Trust will take immediate action, legal if necessary, to stop further damage and correct the problem. When there are new owners of the land, or when questions arise about the easement, the staff will spend the time to ensure the landowner's understanding of the easement. Some easements have provisions for site review and approval by the grantee, also requiring added staff and possibly legal time.

To cover its monitoring, servicing, and enforcement costs, the Trust requests each easement donor to make a one-time, tax-deductible contribution to the Stewardship Fund. The amount is based on an estimate of the staff time, mileage, and legal services needed to monitor, service, and enforce the easement. The money is placed into an endowment fund whose use is restricted to the monitoring, management, and enforcement activities for all Trust properties. If a violation occurs, the Trust has available the entire amount of the fund to support whatever enforcement action is needed. An endowment gift is not required for the Trust to accept an easement, although the Trustees will consider this in their decision making.

In effect, the Stewardship Fund is an insurance policy providing security to the easement donor and the Trust that the land will be protected forever. The donor's contribution is the premium.

If the Trust accepts an executory ("backup") interest in a conservation easement, staff will write to the primary holder of the easement each year to request written confirmation that proper monitoring and enforcement have been done. If the primary easement holder fails to carry out these duties, the Trust can assume the associated responsibilities, and costs. As the backup party, the Trust requests an endowment contribution that is half of what it would request if it were the primary easement holder. Such funds help cover the costs of the Trust's role as backup, and the costs of monitoring, servicing, and enforcement if the Trust ever assumes the easement.

EXAMPLE OF ENDOWMENT CONTRIBUTION CALCULATION

Assume: Conservation easement on 100-acre parcel near downtown Wolfeboro

Monitoring

56 mi. rnd. trip from Meredith @ $.25/mi.	$14.00
3 hrs. staff time @ $16.50/hr.	49.50
Total annual monitoring cost	$63.50

Servicing Landowner Questions/Issues

1 hr. staff time per yr. @ $16.50	16.50

Enforcement

Assume: One problem per 20 yrs., requiring 6 hrs. of both attorney and staff time.

6 hrs. atty. @ $80/hr.	$480.00
6 hrs. staff @ $16.50/hr.	99.00
Total enforcement costs per 20 yrs.	$579.00
Total annual enforcement costs ($579/20)	$28.95
Total annual monitoring and enforcement costs	$108.95

Contribution Calculation

Assume: 7% interest on investment, with interest of 4% retained annually as new principal to prevent inflationary erosion of endowment's value. Therefore, what sum will generate interest of 3% (7% - 4%) annually, equalling $108.95?

3% x $3,632 = $108.95

TOTAL ENDOWMENT CONTRIBUTION REQUESTED

As Holder Of Primary Interest = $3,532

As Holder Of Executory (Backup) Interest = $3,082 x .5 = $1,816

APPENDIX J

(Continued)

POLICY ON STEWARDSHIP ENDOWMENT CONTRIBUTIONS

(from the Vermont Land Trust)

In accepting gifts of conservation restrictions, the Vermont Land Trust (VLT) takes on stewardship responsibilities which insure the integrity and terms of the conservation restriction are not violated. These stewardship responsibilities include monitoring and enforcement of the terms of the restrictions over time. These are permanent responsibilities which VLT must have the capability to perform 10, 20, even 100 or 200 years into the future. As a result, VLT asks that each donor of conservation restrictions donate a cash endowment sufficient to cover VLT's responsibilities and potential liabilities. This endowment insures that VLT will be able to honor its commitment to monitor and enforce the terms of the easement so that many years after the current property owners have departed, their conservation actions will still be in full force and effect. The endowment contributions are deposited in a separate stewardship account which is available only to meet the costs of the stewardship program.

The endowment contribution covers four principal functions:

1. **Documentation.** The Trust prepares a Land Use Documentation Report documenting man-made structures, vegetative cover (fields, forest and any unique flora or fauna), land use history, and distinct natural features. Topographic and aerial base maps of the property are prepared along with a detailed boundary map if a survey does not exist. On-site photos, signed and numbered with photo points mapped, are also taken. This Report is signed by both the landowner and the Trust, and the landowner will have a copy to keep.
2. **Monitoring.** The endowment covers the cost of future monitoring visits to the protected property, which should be accomplished on an annual basis. The monitoring visits may be accomplished either through on-ground visits by VLT staff and volunteers or through an aerial flyover.
3. **Legal Defense.** A portion of the endowment contribution builds VLT's legal defense capability. Over time there are bound to be some violations of conservation restrictions held by VLT. Most will be settled through voluntary means. However, VLT must be prepared to defend the restrictions through litigation, if that is necessary.
4. **Inflation Adjustment.** A portion of the endowment insures that VLT

will be able to meet its future stewardship responsibilities in light of increased costs and the effects of inflation. As a result, the endowment should grow by at least the rate of inflation so that VLT will be able to maintain and enhance its monitoring and enforcement capacity.

Ensuring that the VLT has the capacity to meet its future responsibilities has a direct bearing on preserving the integrity of conservation restrictions. With regard to the actual costs of monitoring, between a half day and a full day may be required to set up the visit, travel to and from a site, and conduct the monitoring. At today's rates, this costs between $200 and $400 of direct cost to the Trust to perform the monitoring function. Using an investment return rate of 5.5% (after adjustment for inflation), an endowment fund of between $3,500 and $7,000 is needed to cover this expense.

The following chart quantifies endowment contributions for different properties based on the two most critical factors: size and number of reserved lots. Obviously, the larger the size of the property, the more time needed to conduct and prepare for the monitoring visit. In addition, the number of reserved housesites adds significantly to the complexity and number of people involved in a particular project, which increases the potential for misunderstanding. As a result, the number of reserved housesites that need to be monitored has a significant impact on the amount of time and effort necessary to conduct a monitoring visit.

Endowment by Property Size and Number of Reserved Housesites

(includes $600 Documentation Cost)

	# of housesites				
Acres	**0-1**	**2**	**3**	**4**	**5+**
<25	$2,600	$3,000	$3,200	$3,800	
26-99	3,600	4,400	4,200	4,800	case
100-299	4,600	5,400	5,200	5,800	by
300-499	5,600	6,400	6,200	6,800	case
500-699	6,600	7,400	7,200	7,800	
Over 700	determined on a case-by-case basis				

If VLT co-holds the restrictions with another entity, which requires more administration and reporting to be performed by VLT, the rate is increased

APPENDIX J

(Continued)

$500. Some uses of the land protected by the conservation restrictions require Trust review and approval, such as the construction of a new housesite. Many of these approvals can be handled during the course of a regular monitoring visit. However, if VLT is asked to make a special visit to the property, VLT reserves the right to bill the owner for its staff time and out-of-pocket expenses.

Endowment contributions are usually due at the time that conservation restrictions are granted (*i.e.,* the closing) since VLT's responsibilities and liability commence at that point. However, if this is not possible, the landowner is asked to sign a pledge agreement to pay the endowment over a period of time. In instances where the application of the endowment contribution schedule will cause an undue hardship on the donor, the Trust's Board of Trustees may, at its discretion, lower or waive the endowment requirement.

Gifts of Land in Fee

With regard to calculating endowments for gifts of land donated in fee in which the trust will retain ownership, the endowment must be sufficient to cover the Trust's actual and anticipated annual operating costs. These costs will have to be calculated on a case-by-case basis in cooperation with the landowner because the varying management objectives and annual carrying costs such as property taxes. The Trust's Board of Trustees will review each gift of land and the endowment fee.

For gifts of land that will subsequently be resold by the Trust, there is generally no need for an endowment contribution from the donor. The Trust's costs will be covered from the proceeds of the subsequent resale. The Board of Trustees will review all proposed gifts of land.

Baseline Documentation

For each acquisition of land or conservation restrictions the Trust must prepare a baseline data file on the property being protected. Not only is this documentation good policy, baseline data is an IRS requirement for landowners claiming an income tax deduction. The endowment contribution described above includes $600 for baseline documentation.

In certain instances where the landowner already has or can obtain detailed land use information, the contribution for baseline documentation may be lowered.

APPENDIX K
Sample Amendment Policy

POLICY ON AMENDING CONSERVATION RESTRICTIONS
(from the Vermont Land Trust)

General Statement of Policy

The Vermont Land Trust acquires and holds conservation restrictions in property in order to protect agricultural, forestry, wildlife, ecological, recreational and open space values for the benefit of present and future generations of Vermonters.

Because its acquisitions are accomplished through voluntary agreements with landowners, the success of the program depends upon the confidence of these owners that the Trust will meet its obligation to monitor and enforce the agreements. This confidence would be seriously eroded if the Vermont Land Trust allowed modification of its conservation agreements. Amendments could also raise potential problems with the Internal Revenue Service, both for the Trust in terms of its tax-exempt status and for donors of conservation restrictions in terms of any charitable deduction that may have been claimed for a gift.

Therefore, it is the policy of the Vermont Land Trust to hold and enforce its conservation agreements as written. As such, it will permit amendments to conservation restrictions only in very exceptional circumstances. Any request for an amendment will be reviewed according to the procedures set forth in this Policy Statement, and will be implemented only where the Board of Trustees determines that:

(1) the requested modification is warranted under one or more of the purposes set forth below;

(2) it is the minimum change necessary to satisfy that purpose; and

(3) it will not erode the confidence of the Trust's supporters—including both past and future donors of conservation restrictions and other interests in land—about the goals of the organization or its intent to enforce its conservation agreements.

Additionally, unless specifically waived by the Board of Trustees, the requestor shall pay all staff costs pertaining to reviewing the change, whether or not the request is approved, and if approved, to its implementation.

Purpose of Requested Amendment

The Vermont Land Trust will consider modification to its conservation restrictions only in the following circumstances:

(continued)

APPENDIX K

(Continued)

1. **Prior Agreement.** In a few cases, a conservation agreement has included a specific provision allowing modification of the restrictions at a future date under specified circumstances. Such agreements must be set forth in the conservation restriction document or in a separate document signed by both parties at the time the conservation agreement was executed. The amendment must be consistent with the terms and conservation intent of the original agreement.
2. **Correction of an Error or Ambiguity.** The Vermont Land Trust may authorize an amendment to correct an obvious error or oversight made at the time the conservation restrictions were entered into. This may include correction of a legal description, inclusion of standard language that was unintentionally omitted, or clarification of an ambiguity in the terms of the restrictions in order to avoid litigation over the interpretation of the document in the future.
3. **Settlement of Condemnation Proceedings.** Conservation restrictions and other interests the Vermont Land Trust holds in land use are subject to condemnation for public purposes, such as highways, schools, etc. Where it appears that the condemnation power would be properly exercised, the Trust may enter into a settlement agreement with the condemning authority in order to avoid the expense of litigation. In reaching such an agreement, the Trust shall attempt to preserve the intent of the original conservation agreement to the greatest extent possible.
4. **Minor Modifications Consistent with Conservation Purpose.** The Trust may authorize other, minor modifications of the conservation restrictions where (a) the modification is not inconsistent with the intent of the principal parties to the original conservation project, and (b) the amended agreement is substantially equivalent to or enhances the conservation goals of the original agreement.

   The Board of Trustees will be extremely cautious in consenting to a change under this section, and will do so only where the circumstances suggest that a change is clearly warranted and in the best interests of conservation. For example, the Trust may deed, in the form of an amended agreement, "anchor parcels" back to the landowners, where the anchor parcel was acquired to ensure the enforceability of conservation restrictions prior to a change in Vermont law. In another case, the Trust may allow the change of a housesite permitted under the conservation restrictions to a new

(continued)

location, where the new location has a lower impact on the conservation values sought to be protected under the restrictions. No change will be made to allow for an additional housesite not provided for under the original agreement.

Procedures for Requesting an Amendment

Any landowner seeking a modification to an existing conservation agreement shall file a request in writing with the Trust stating what change is being sought and the specific reasons why it is needed or warranted. Where appropriate, the request shall also be accompanied by a map and other documentation. Unless waived, the request shall also be accompanied by a payment of $500 to cover the Trust's staff costs. Any unexpended portion of the fee shall be refunded, and the landowner shall be responsible for all costs exceeding the initial fee.

The President shall review all requests and, where appropriate, shall refer them to the Trust's field staff for an evaluation, a site visit and recommendation. The field review shall include reasonable efforts to contact the principal parties to the original transaction, including the landowner who donated/sold the restrictions, any town or State board or agency which contributed funds to the acquisition, and any persons who supported the acquisition through financial gifts, pledges of charitable credit, etc.

The field staff shall present all of the information thus gathered, together with its recommendation, to a panel consisting of the Trust's President, Stewardship Director and General Counsel. If the panel concludes that the amendment is legally permissible, consistent with the terms of this Policy Statement, and clearly warranted by the circumstances, the President shall forward the request and staff recommendation to the Board of Trustees. A decision of the panel to disapprove the request shall be final, unless the landowner requests further review by the Board of Trustees.

The Board of Trustees may approve, approve with modification, or reject the request for amendment at its next regularly scheduled meeting or at a special meeting warned for that purpose. Approval shall require a majority vote of the full Board of Trustees.

APPENDIX L
Resources

The following publications, journals, and videos are available from the Land Trust Alliance. Call for current prices.

Appraising Easements: Guidelines for the Valuation of Historic Preservation and Land Conservation Easements, second edition. 1990. Land Trust Alliance and the National Trust for Historic Preservation, Washington, DC. This comprehensive guide was prepared by expert appraisers and lawyers and is used by government agencies and non-profit organizations that acquire easements, as well as by appraisers and landowners.

The Back Forty: the Newsletter of Land Conservation Law. 1990-present. Published by the Land Conservation Law Institute, a project of the Land Trust Alliance and Hastings College of the Law, University of California. Written especially for land conservation practitioners and their legal advisors, *The Back Forty* is published 10 times a year. Relevant topics that have been covered include "Easements in the Wake of Catastrophe: The Legal Fallout" (April 1991); "Recent Easement Amendment Survey Findings" (March 1991); "Conservation Easements and the Doctrine of Changed Conditions" (July/August 1990); "What Must the Taking Authority Pay for Land Subject to a Conservation Easement?" (July/August 1990 and September 1990); "Extinguishment of Easements: 'Division of Proceeds' Clauses" (June 1990).

The Conservation Easement Handbook: Managing Land Conservation and Historic Preservation Easement Programs, by Janet Diehl and Thomas S. Barrett, Esq. 1988. Land Trust Alliance and the Trust for Public Land, Washington, DC. Written by the leading experts in the field, this comprehensive guide is an essential resource for any organization that intends to handle easements. Includes model easements with explanatory legal commentary.

Exchange: The Journal of the Land Trust Alliance. 1982-present. Land Trust Alliance, Washington, DC. The professional journal of the land trust movement, published four times a year. Most issues feature special topics. Relevant issues include "Land Trust Liability and Risk

Management" (Winter 1991); "Appraising Conservation Easements" (Summer 1990); "Land Trusts and Hazardous Wastes" (Summer 1989); "Conservation Easements," with stories on violations, condemnation, and mortgage subordination (Spring 1989).

The Federal Tax Law of Conservation Easements with *1986-1988 Supplement,* by Stephen J. Small, Esq. 1986, 1989. Land Trust Alliance, Washington, DC. This is the authoritative guide to the subject, written by the attorney who prepared the draft of the easement regulations for the IRS. It includes a history and interpretation of the regulations, discussions of related income and estate taxes, and copies of the statute, letter rulings, and revenue rulings.

"For the Common Good: Preserving Private Lands with Conservation Easements." 1985. Land Trust Alliance, Washington, DC. This award-winning, 16-minute video is a clear, persuasive portrayal of the public benefits being achieved through conservation easements. Ideally suited for showing to public officials, landowners, and groups interested in learning about the work of land trusts.

Preserving Family Lands: A Landowner's Introduction to Tax Issues and Other Considerations, by Stephen J. Small, Esq. 1988. Powers & Hall, Boston. An easy-to-understand, readable booklet warning landowners that estate taxes may force their heirs to sell the family's land for development, and describing potential ways to conserve the land, reduce estate taxes, and keep the land in the family.

Statement of Land Trust Standards & Practices. 1989. Land Trust Alliance, Washington, DC. This booklet outlines the standards and practices that the Land Trust Alliance believes are essential for the responsible operation of a land trust.